KINGTONES
1964
Memoirs

To Karen & Bob,

Let the good times roll!

Bruce M. Snoop

Oct. 22, 2013

KINGTONES
1964 Memoirs

By Bruce Snoap

Published by Bruce Snoap

Kingtones Memoirs –1964
by Bruce Snoap
Copyright © 2012 by Bruce Snoap

All rights reserved. No part of this book may be reproduced in any form or by any electronic or mechanical means including information storage and retrieval systems without permission in writing from Bruce Snoap.

Editor in Chief: Laura Beth Snoap
Consultant Editor: Bruce Snoap II
Associate Editor, Foreword: Kim Rush
Cover and book design: Joe Mercier

Published by Bruce Snoap
595 Westway Dr. N.W.
Grand Rapids, MI 49534

ISBN 978-0-9886003-0-0

First Printing, March 2013
Printed and bound in the United States of America

1964 2012

This Book is dedicated to my high school sweetheart and wife,
Chick Snoap, for her unconditional devotion and love for
over 50 years; For three wonderful children and a
smile that still lights up my life; For her patience
in putting up with the Kingtones for 45 years.

Contents

Foreword xi
Introduction xiii
Day One: Problems, Mishaps and Mistakes (February 6) 15
"Welcome to Florida" (February 7) 16
"Keep a Knockin' But You Can't Come In" (February 8) 17
Daytona Beach, Sucktastic! (February 8) 17
Running a Teenage Nightclub? (February 9) 18
Beatles Play the Ed Sullivan Show (February 9) 18
Miami via Cocoa Beach (February 10) 20
Bob Gets Pulled over (February 10) 20
Captain Joe's Strip Club (February 11) 21
Porky's, Here We Come (February 11) 22
Plantation Apartments (February 12) 23
The Beatles Invade Miami (February 13) 24
"Fog" and the Valentine's Party (February 14) 26
Lloyd Becomes a Mentor (February 15) 26
Beatles on TV; Lloyd to the Rescue (February 16) 27
Bob & Phil Look for Work; Universal Portrait (February 17) 28
Bitch, Complain, Criticize, Whine (February 18) 29
Oh Woe is Me, "Cook Your Own Meal!" (February 19) 30
Getting Along Fine; the "Puppet Master" is Out (February 20) 31
Union "Blocks" The Kingtones (February 21) 31
Lloyd Saves the Day (February 22) 32
Chick is Coming! (February 23) 33
Union Contracts Arrive (February 24) 34
Cassius Clay/Sonny Liston Fight (February 25) 35
Porky's Dictatorship (February 26) 36
Audition for "Invisible Man" (February 27) 37
Kingtones to Miami (February 28) 38
Bruce, Designated Leader for Ten Minutes (February 28) 38
Experimental Cooking Voted Worst Meal's Ever (February 29) 39
"Bob the Blob" (March 1) 40
First Day at Porky's (March 2) 41

Measles Keeps Mike Isolated (March 2)	41
Mike Meets Jellyfish! (March 3)	43
Gee, Porky Seemed So Nice at First (March 4)	44
Finding a Place for Family to Stay (March 5)	44
Phil's Amp Stops; Pete Goes Hoarse (March 6)	45
Chick Arrives (March 7)	46
Porky Says "Yes" to Underage Girlfriend (March 8)	47
A Renewed Frame of Mind (March 9)	48
Bob Rents His Car to Bruce (March 10)	49
Chick's Last Day; Phil Passes Out (March 11)	49
MediQuick to the Rescue (March 11)	49
"One Band's Loss Is Another Band's Gain" (March 12)	51
Special Musical Group, the Treniers (March 13)	52
Lloyd Invites Band (March 14)	53
Soulmen Are Big Hit; Goodbye Thunderbirds (March 15)	54
Kingtones Name in Lights (March 16)	55
Playing Only Rock 'n Roll Mesmerizes Audience (March 17)	56
"Kingtones Sound" Emerges (March 18)	57
Kingtones Fifth Record Released on West Coast (March 19)	58
"The Calm before the Storm" (March 19)	58
Porky's Pirate Ship (March 20)	59
Mike's Girl Plays "Keep Away" (March 20)	59
"The Situations" (March 21)	61
Dave Roberts Turns Mediocre Night into Good Night (March 21)	61
89 Cent Fishing Poles; College Students Arrive (March 22)	62
MSU Landing, Mass Hysteria (March 23)	63
Lenny Wants Kingtones; "Chinese Sweatshop" in the Making (March 23)	63
Musician's Union Work Dues (March 24)	65
Mike Gets Drunk; The Percussions Start (March 25)	66
Elvis Is In The Building: (March 25)	66
Pete Claims "Home Run" (March 25)	66
Jam Session "Savages" (March 26)	68
The Thrill of Victory and the Agony (March 26)	68
"Joe Crudface" (March 27)	70
Excited to Crazy (March 27)	70
Guys Create Contest Challenges (March 28)	71

African Beatles Are Big Hit (March 28) 71
Spring Break Almost Over (March 29) 72
African Beatles Not Allowed to Perform (March 29) 72
Pete "Trades" Bob for Phil (March 29) 72
The Percussions Jam; Kingtones Visit Killer Whales (March 30) 74
"Elvis" Causes Pandemonium at Porky's (March 30) 74
Airline Stewardess (March 30) 74
A Meal Fit for a King-*tone* (March 31) 76
Bruce Becomes "Birdman" (March 31) 76
"The Bird," Our Golden Egg Flops (April 1) 78
Homer Says Good-Bye (April 1) 78
Landlord Wants Kingtones Out (April 2) 79
Frank, One of the Best (April 2) 79
Strangers in Our Apartment (April 2) 79
Pete and Phil Get Ousted by Girl's Landlord (April 3) 81
22 Caliber Pistol; Bob Dates "Chubby" (April 3) 81
Girl of His Dreams (April 4) 82
Bar Fight Clears Club (April 4) 82
Porky Drops One Night and Pay (April 4) 82
Kingtones Name Comes Down (April 5) 84
African Beatles Now Featured (April 5) 84
Monkey Jungle Visited (April 6) 85
"Kingtones Sound" Disappears; Last Night at Porky's (April 6) 85
Bruce Receives Surfin' Bird "Trophy" (April 7) 86
Apollos Start at Porky's (April 7) 86
The Take Off, The Crash (April 8) 87
Phil Fails as Car Thief (April 8) 87
Mashed Potato Sandwiches? (April 9) 89
Our Last "Hurrah" (April 9) 89
Atlanta, Georgia – "Wild Man's Land" (April 10) 90
$4.00 Tire Fixes Shimmy (April 11) 90
Vending Machine Restaurant (April 11) 90
Engine on Fire (April 11) 90
Where Are They Now? 93
Kingtoneisms 96
Pictures and Memorabilia 98

KINGTONES MEMOIRS – 1964

Foreword

I was a fan of the popular local rock and roll band from Grand Rapids, Michigan called the Kingtones. They formed in the late 1950s when they were teenagers. They played at dances, local bars and nightclubs as well as the teenage "nightclubs" which were popular in Michigan in the '60s. They were fortunate to occasionally back up and perform at the same venues with national acts like Bobby Vinton, Del Shannon, Bobby Vee and the Beach Boys. They recorded their music in local recording studios; their records were played and promoted by local DJs and they experienced some minor brushes with recording fame.

In 1964 the Kingtones were packing the clubs in West Michigan. They were also performing at a chain of nightclubs called Coral Gables around the state. In Lansing, the Coral Gables nightclub added three additions to their original building to accommodate the huge crowds they were drawing! They had also just released a successful single called *Twins* that was being played regularly on the radio; they had received an offer to issue it on a national label. As a result, they were very encouraged and excited about their recent successes, and figured they could take the band down to Florida during spring break and find a job playing in a nightclub. Without a secured engagement waiting for them in Florida, they packed their equipment in their van and drove to Florida, in pursuit of fun, adventure and the opportunity to perform for the kids during Spring break!

This story manuscript provides an inside view of a small but intriguing portion of the Kingtones fifty year career. It is actually the contents of Bruce Snoap's diary entries from the 10 week trip the Kingtones made to Florida in the winter/spring of 1964. All the band members had watched the 1960 movie, *Where the Boys Are* and wanted to personally experience the excitement of the college spring break season in Florida. After a number of disappointments, while scrambling hard to find work, they finally ended up playing at one of the hottest nightclubs in Fort Lauderdale: Porky's.

The storyline includes details of their eventful trip down to Florida, the struggle to find work for the band and pay for food and expenses, the amusing interaction of the band members who lived together in close quarters in cheap motel rooms and a small apartment, and the final relief and triumph of finding a place to work.

It is likely that numerous musicians who played in rock and roll bands in the 1960s can relate to this plot. However, I believe that people from all age groups, ranging from high school students to senior citizens, may identify with the story, and will enjoy getting an inside look at the struggles and successes of five young men who were trying to be great, if only for a short time. The camaraderie, the girlfriends, the fights, the rejections, the laughter and the thrill of eventual triumph are all here.

Kim Rush (Historian & Friend of Bruce Snoap)

Co-Creator/Editor
West Michigan Music Hysterical Society Website
www.westmichmusichystericalsociety.com/

Introduction

The hair on my head is much thinner now and has changed color. My nice smooth skin is now wrinkled and I don't see or hear like I use to. I can only remember flashes of that time. It is now the 21st Century, 2013. February 6, 1964 seems like an eternity ago. I do have my diary however, that can help me go back, back to The Kingtones adventures of going to Ft. Lauderdale, Florida, to play for the college students during spring break. Some of my notes are hard to read and also subject to interpretation, but I will try to make this period of time in our lives as accurate as possible.

Of the five boys that were in The Kingtones at that time, four of them are still with us. Only the lead singer, Pete Mervenne has passed away. But this book is not about The Kingtones later years; It is about a 10 week period of time in the lives of five young boys in a band and their quest to experience being heard, in the hottest Spring Break destination of that time, Fort Lauderdale, Florida.

Bruce Snoap

February 6, 1964 (Thursday)

In our quest for national recognition and in fulfilling our contractual recording agreement with Cadet Distributing of Detroit, the Kingtones met at the Our Theater in Grand Rapids, Michigan, to finish up our next record release. Dave Kalmbach, owner and recording engineer of Fenton Records, met us there at 6:00 am. We were so excited about going to Ft. Lauderdale, that it was hard to stay focused on the recording session. We just had to do a couple more recordings before we could leave. We were all packed and ready to go. At 8:30 am, we were finished with the recordings and thus our journey to Fort Lauderdale began.

Pete Mervenne (lead singer – age 20), Mike King (drummer – age 18) and I (Bruce Snoap – keyboards, age 20; turned 21 Feb. 13), drove The Kingtones' van with the band equipment in it. Phil Roberts (lead guitar – age 20), followed in his 1955 yucky gold Thunderbird; Bob Major (bass player – age 20), drove his 1957 "cherry condition" silver convertible Oldsmobile '98.

Our excitement was soon squelched by the long monotonous drive, the rain that lasted all day, no sunshine to lift our spirits and a series of problems, mishaps, mistakes, etc. that we encountered. Making a right turn instead of a left and going 22 miles out of the way, was just the beginning. Although most of us thought this to be a little funny, Bob was pissed; after all, he had to pay for his own gas. As we proceeded, Phil got a flat tire, had an oil leak and his windshield wipers broke. Pete, who was driving the van, laughed so hard about Phil's car problems, he missed his turn off. Upon realizing this, he stopped the van to turn around and got stuck in the soft shoulder mud. Bob, with his big Oldsmobile, pushed the van out. Mike, Pete and I pushed on the side of the van so it wouldn't tip over. Although Major, was able to push the van out, he managed to put a nice dent in the back of it.

Financing for this wild and crazy adventure was basically "every man for himself." We did have a "kitty," that Phil was in charge of that everyone had to put in $40.00 to start with. This money would be used for band expenses: gas, oil, groceries, rent, etc… Other than that, you were on your own.

Not having a lot of money, my mother packed a box full of "Grandma's Fried Chicken" for all of us to eat. Continuing on our journey, we finished the chicken and threw the box out the window to make more room in the already cramped van. Somehow, one of my shoes had gotten in the box.

When we finally realized that we threw one of my shoes out the window, we were a couple hundred miles down the road; we weren't going back in hopes of finding it.

Rotating drivers to help ward off fatigue was working fine and kept us moving towards our destination. Mike, nicknamed "Clod" because of all the times he hurt himself, broke things, screwed things up etc., took over driving for Phil. Mike wanted to impress Pete and me by showing how fast he could take off with Phil's car which temporarily broke Phil's gas pedal. To add to our frustration, we lost Bob Major for about half an hour because we took a wrong road while Bob took the correct one.

At 7:00 pm we stopped for dinner. The food was absolutely terrible. I got sick because of it. Since we had so little money, we decided to "put the pedal to the metal" and drive straight through to Florida to save on one nights lodging. So Pete (alias Mario Andretti) in the Kingtones' van, Phil (alias A.J. Foyt) driving his "cool" T-Bird and Mike (alias Richard Petty) driving Bob's "OLDS 98", took the wheel and were off like jets. It wasn't long before a red flashing light was seen in the rear view mirror. All three drivers were pulled over and given tickets. The Sheriff made us all follow him to the Justice of the Peace to pay the fines. They wouldn't let us go until we came up with the money. The three "Race Drivers" had to pay $17.50 each. This left Pete with $9.00 to his name to survive in Florida. Our first day's experience on the road seemed like the longest day and night in the history of travel.

February 7, 1964 (Friday)

With the rising of the sun and the fresh smell of oranges in the air, our spirits once again became very excited, especially when we saw the sign: *Welcome to Florida – the Sunshine State*. Wow! It was about 10:30 am and just a beautiful day. All the car windows were down and Bob and Phil put their car tops down. It was nice and warm outside with not a cloud in the sky.

We stopped for breakfast. This time the food was delicious. Everything seemed better. We were laughing, joking and getting along quite well. We even ignored Mike when he gave us this stupid grin, like the cat that ate the canary and started beating on his chest like King Kong because he had been driving Phil's T-Bird. After breakfast we started for Orlando. We arrived there around 5:30 p.m. We were exhausted! Tired! Beat! Pooped! You name it and we were it.

We decided to get a motel and crash for the night. We stopped at three different motels. The first one looked like a dump. We didn't really care as long as it was cheap. They wanted $15.00 for the room! We couldn't believe how expensive this "dump" was. We left and found another motel. This looked a little better than the first one, but since they wanted $14.00 for the night, and we didn't have much money, we decided to try one more place. On our third attempt, we struck gold. We almost didn't stop because it was a much nicer place than its predecessors and we figured it would cost a fortune. But since we were so tired, we thought we'd give it a try. They were asking $12.00 for the night! Hallelujah! Our prayers had been answered! We certainly didn't understand why the room was so cheap, but we didn't care.

After getting into the room, we realized we were right next to a very busy highway. We could hear everything. If we weren't so tired, we probably would have been awake all night. But as tired as we were we closed our eyes and didn't move until morning.

February 8, 1964 (Saturday)

Being as tired as we were, none of us got up until 11:50 am. Since check out time was noon, we dressed as quickly as we could and ran out the door to our vehicles: no showers, no shaving, no brushing our teeth, nothing! We didn't want to pay for an extra night.

Our mission for the day was to go knocking on night club doors, tell them we would like to audition for them, and have them say "Come right in, set up on the stage over there….. You guys are Great! You're hired!" Then we could go find a place to stay and rent it for a few weeks. Well, it didn't go exactly as planned. Little Richard's song *"Keep a Knockin' But You Can't Come In,"* started to have a whole new meaning to us. Every club we tried to audition for either didn't have live bands or were happy with the band they had and they wouldn't even listen to us.

After a few hours of being turned away, we decided to go to Daytona to try our luck. "Clod" (Mike), read the map wrong and we went way out of our way, adding an extra 50 minutes to our travel time. Adding to our frustration already was the fact that we almost lost Major again.

Daytona had a lot of clubs that used bands. The problems we encountered here were similar to the ones we had in Orlando. They liked the band they had, and they wouldn't let us audition. They also had contracts with these bands and couldn't hire us even if they wanted to. This was a dilemma we had never thought about.

We finally found a club that was going to attempt teenage dances. Charlie, the manager, did not have a band yet and was anxious to hear us. In fact, he wasn't officially even open. But, he said if we wanted to set up and audition, and if he liked us, he would open the club that night. He offered to pay us $25.00 and we could sleep in the club after we were done playing. Since we had little to no money, we figured "Hey, $25.00 would help buy gas and some food." And having a place to stay would save us one night's lodging.

Of course, there was no advertisement for the club and no one even knew that it existed at that time, but you know the old saying, "Never look a gift horse in the mouth." So we set up our equipment and did the audition. The acoustics were not very good and WE thought we stunk. Charlie however liked us, so our first job had been secured.

When it came time to start playing, a few teenagers who had been walking down the street and saw this teenage nightclub open, stopped in. We played to an almost empty room. Phil had made some equipment adjustments and our sound was halfway decent. When we finished playing and it was time for bed, we found out our "bed" was the floor. To add to this exciting news, Phil had lost his wallet for a short time, giving us all "heart failure" because all of the Kingtones "Kitty" money was in it.

We were getting along about as well as could be expected considering all of our failures, rejections and disappointments. We were very tired of traveling. It had been a long day and tomorrow looked like it would be more of the same. Daytona was a great city and we would have loved to have played there, but things weren't settled here so it looked like we were going to have to continue traveling further south if we hoped to find work. Maybe we would have better luck in Cocoa Beach; we were going to try there on Monday. As I lay on my "nice wooden floor bed," with socks for a pillow and my coat for a blanket, my misery was temporarily relieved with thoughts of Chick, my girlfriend back in Michigan.

February 9, 1964 (Sunday)

Since our sleeping accommodations were not exactly the best, we did not sleep very well. To make matters worse, we woke up in the middle of the night shivering. It was one of Florida's coldest nights in years. Someone decided to rectify the situation and turned the thermostat up. After about a half an hour we were frozen. The "Helpful Kingtone" who thought he had turned the furnace up actually turned the air conditioner on. What a night!

Needless to say, we were up nice and early. Since we were all starved, we headed down the street to eat breakfast at a highly recommended restaurant. The thought of a nice warm room quickened our pace. The food there was really good, but boy was it expensive! It cost me $2.20 for my breakfast. (I was used to eating at Perkins Restaurant in Grand Rapids, where I could get 2 eggs, toast and coffee for 65 cents.) We figured that the restaurant must be a favorite eating place for high rollers.

Charlie wanted us to play Sunday night. He said he would pay us $55.00. He also mentioned that maybe, if he could talk his boss into it, and if we were interested, the Kingtones could take over and run the club. We got the feeling that the running of a teenage night club was not Charlie's "Cup of Tea." He was only attempting to run this club, because his boss told him to.

So we hung around the club all day Sunday. We talked about the pros and cons of running a teenage night club. It was an awful risk, but on the other hand it could pay off very well. We did a little practicing in the afternoon and Phil fixed some of the equipment that needed fine tuning.

We decided that since there was a motel right across the street from the club, with an efficiency kitchen, that we would stay there for the night. We didn't want to sleep on the floor again. Besides, I enjoyed cooking, and with a kitchen I could cook some meals... saving us money. But the big reason we really wanted the room was because it had a television set. The teenage night club did not have one. We wanted a television, because one of the most important events in the history of rock music was going to be aired at 8:00 pm on the Ed Sullivan Show. The Beatles were making their first American television appearance that night. They came on at 8:00 pm and again at 8:35 pm. We wanted to be a part of the 73 million viewers to witness that historic event.

After watching the Beatles, we were excited about playing. We knew several Beatle songs and were anxious to show our audience how well we could play them. Audience? What audience? There was almost no one there. It was like playing in a ghost town at the "Ghost Bar".

When we finished playing, we headed across the street to get a good night sleep. Everyone was still healthy, in spite of the fact that we froze last night: "coldest weather in months," people were saying. Before I went to bed, I cleaned up the dinner dishes. I was shocked, when Bob offered to wipe them. I figured that he must want something from me. In the morning we were going to meet Charlie's boss and talk to him about running the Teenage Club. I wanted to write Chick. I thought about her constantly and missed her. But as soon as I finished my daily journal writing I passed out.

February 10, 1964 (Monday)

We got up around 11:00 am. We were excited about meeting Charlie's boss and excited about the possibility of running our own teenage night club. I cooked breakfast, cleaned up and we all headed over to the club. I don't really remember what was said at the meeting, but what I do know is that the Boss Man said, "No!" He didn't want us to run his club.

Charlie felt very bad for us and probably for himself as well. He could see how disappointed we were. To try and make us feel better, he said that he had a friend in Miami, Captain Joe, who owned his own night club. He offered to call him, on our behalf, to see if he could get us an audition there. Captain Joe said that he would listen to us, and if we were any good, we could start playing for him Tuesday night, Feb. 11.

So we departed Charlie and Daytona Beach and headed for Miami. On our way, we decided to stop in Cocoa Beach and try our luck at getting a job there. One of the most popular clubs that had dance music in Cocoa Beach was the Satellite Bar. We stopped in and found the house band about ready to practice. We struck up a conversation with them. That's when we discovered that if you didn't have a Union Contract to play at a club, you probably would not be allowed to play there. It was now around supper time, so we decided to go get a bite to eat. The band members from the Satellite joined us. When we were finished eating, they asked us to come back to the bar with them to hear a few of their tunes...so we did. They were actually a pretty good rock band.

We finally got back on the road to Miami around 8:00 pm. Since the three of our vehicles always followed each other, whoever was the "lead car" had to constantly check his rearview mirror to make sure everybody was there. After traveling for a while, the driver noticed that there was only one car behind him instead of two; we lost Phil. We turned around and went looking for him. We finally found him with his second flat tire; he had no spare.

We had passed a gas station several miles back, so we took Phil's flat tire to get it fixed. While they were fixing it, I called Chick on a pay phone. It cost me a fortune, but just hearing her voice made me happy. I really missed her. We took the fixed tire back to Phil. While he put the tire on his car, Pete, Bob and I decided to walk a wooden fence that was close by. Pete and Bob took their time and walked from one fence post to the next. I was going to show them that I could do it in half the time. As I started walking with an accelerated pace, I slipped, fell, cracked the fence rail and "creamed" my arm. Even though Pete and Bob acted concerned about my fall, their laughter and snickering made me think that they really didn't care.

When we finally got back on the road, Bob took the lead. He was tired of how long it was taking us to get to Miami, and wanted to make up for lost time. He took off before we even got into our vehicles. We finally caught up with him because a cop had pulled him over for speeding. We couldn't believe that Bob didn't get a ticket. He told the police officer that he was a Police Cadet from Grand Rapids, Michigan. As a "Professional Courtesy," he just gave Bob a warning.

What a long day! Just when we thought we couldn't stand it anymore, we drove through Hollywood, FL. We never saw such a beautiful city. The weather and even the smell in the air were spectacular. This, once again, gave us new life and hope.

We finally got to Miami at 3 am. We were beat! The motels there were outrageous in price. They wanted $27.00 and $28.00 for one night. I was able to talk one motel down from $24.00 to $18.00. I stressed the fact that we had already missed half of the night and that it was unlikely that anyone else would be checking in at that late hour. I mentioned that he would be losing money if he didn't accept our offer. We were still getting along okay, but we were starting to get on each other's nerves.

February 11, 1964 (Tuesday)

We got up about 10:30 am. It was a beautiful sunny day, and the temperature was supposed to hit 70. We were very excited about the prospect of getting a job. We all piled into the cars, and headed to Captain Joe's, named after its owner. Upon arriving, we got the surprise of our life. Captain Joe's was a STRIP CLUB!! We started to wonder if we were supposed to play music while the strippers did their thing; if we didn't, when would we play? Would there be any couples there to dance? Or would it be just sex craved men listening to our music, waiting for the strippers to come on stage?

Captain Joe greeted us, fed us lunch (hamburgs), and then let us audition. He liked what he heard and said we could start that night. He would pay us $250.00 for six nights of work. Phil was ready to say yes, when I suggested that since we hadn't even tried the "big clubs" in the Ft. Lauderdale area, and since it was only 21 miles away, that we should go there first to try to audition. I remarked that if we didn't have any luck there, we could make it back to Captain Joe's in 45 minutes and start that night.

Even though Phil was the brains of the group, I hoped a little common sense here, might give us a more favorable outcome. Not knowing what we would be expected to do at Captain Joe's, and the low amount of money he was going to pay us, convinced the guys to at least go and try the clubs in Ft. Lauderdale. There were two very "Hot" and popular night clubs there: Lenny's and Porky's.

Our first stop was Lenny's. Between the two clubs, Lenny's was the biggest and the hottest club in town. This was the place everyone would be going to during spring break. I personally did not like Lenny's. It seemed too big and unfriendly. The owner of the club was not interested in auditioning our band. He already had a band lined up for spring break and didn't want to waste his time listening to us.

Our last stop and last hope was Porky's. The outside of Porky's looked a little run down and old. But when we entered the club, the inside was absolutely beautiful, fabulous, far better than we could have imagined. Donald "Porky" Baines was the owner. Our timing to audition for Porky's was perfect for the both of us. He had just gotten in a big argument with his band and wanted to get rid of them. The band's contract said that Porky could cancel their contract with a two week notice. So we set up our equipment and auditioned. Pete was at the top of his game and the acoustics were good; we sounded Great! Porky loved us. He gave his band their two week notice and told us we could start in two weeks.

What Porky didn't realize when he hired us, was that we had just finished playing at the Coral Gables in Lansing, Michigan. The Coral Gables was remodeled three times while we were playing there to accommodate the huge number of Michigan State students that came to see us. When spring break would come, all those Michigan State kids who would have normally driven past Porky's, on their way to Lenny's, would see "The Kingtones" on Porky's sign and that's all the further they would go. As you will see later on, in the spring of 1964, Porky's became the hottest night club in the Fort Lauderdale area. We believe The Kingtones were the reason why!

One college student, by the name of Bob Clark, who frequented Porky's, years later wrote and produced three movies pertaining to Porky's: Porky's, Porky's II – The Next Day and Porky's Revenge. But that's another story for another time.

We told Porky that we couldn't wait two weeks, because we were almost out of money and we had no where to stay. He said that he owned a houseboat, and we could stay there for a few nights until we found a place. He also said that he would get us a couple one night jobs, to give us a little extra money to tide us over. Since our only other choices seemed to be to go play at Captain Joe's or return to Michigan, we accepted Porky's offer.

We left and found a cheap place for supper. I really wanted to go eat at a restaurant called Mia Kia. It was surrounded with palm trees, flowers, waterfalls, lighted torches and also had beautiful Polynesian waitresses. But on our budget, we couldn't even afford a drink there.

We were starting to NOT get along. We were definitely getting on each other's nerves. We were tired, tired of traveling, felt dirty and needed a little time away from each other; which we probably weren't going to get. We were going to start looking for a place to stay, on Wednesday.

February 12, 1964 (Wednesday)

Porky's houseboat was not very big. It didn't really sleep five people, and only had one blanket per bed. Once again, Florida had "one of the coldest nights in years," and we almost froze. We got up about 10:30 am, got dressed and left immediately to try and find a place to stay. We did not want to stay on that houseboat again. Our goal was to look all day if necessary, until we found some kind of affordable lodging.

The first apartment we looked at was very nice, but they wanted $250.00 a week… so we continued looking. We finally found an apartment; it looked like a converted motel and was about ten miles west of Fort Lauderdale. The name of the community complex was Plantation. We liked the name; it made us feel like we were staying at a place that was big and important. Better yet, we liked the price: $125.00 a week… so we took it. This would be our "home" for the next eight weeks. We got settled in, and relaxed for the first time since we left Michigan. The apartment consisted of a small kitchen, with a small attached living room, a small bedroom and a tiny bathroom.

Tomorrow, we were going to see The Beatles come into the Miami Airport. All of us, that is, except Pete. Our apartment shared a vacant lot with a bar. Pete liked The Beatles, but he liked the Shelazar Bar even more. He had a fake ID, and it was just a short walk to the bar. So he opted out of going to see the most famous rock group of our time, to go and sit at the bar.

We were all healthy and fairly happy. We were getting along a little better today. I took a nice hot shower, since we had no bathtub, ate supper and went to bed.

February 13, 1964 (Thursday)

We got up around 11:00 am. It was my birthday! Bob didn't forget; he said right away, "Happy Birthday!" I went out and bought some ice cream and cake to help celebrate, and also to give the boys a treat.

We were very excited, because The Beatles were coming to Miami today at 4:00 pm. The boys washed their cars, and the four of us, Bob, Mike, Phil and I, departed for Miami. We arrived at the airport around 2:30 pm. By the time we found a parking spot, and got inside the terminal, it was around 3:30 pm. We could hardly open the door to the terminal because there were 7,000 fans already there to greet them. All the viewing decks, windows, outside fences, open spaces, etc. were filled with people. We decided to split up; every man for himself, in our quest to try to see The Beatles!

Mike and I went together. We hadn't gone very far when we saw an elevator door open. On the inside of the elevator, was an ad that said something like… "Come to the seventh floor and relax in our newly remodeled AND EXPENSIVE restaurant. Enjoy the beautiful view from our new picture windows." Hallelujah, our prayers had been answered. Mike and I quickly jumped on the elevator. We didn't want to eat there, we just wanted to look out those big beautiful picture windows, and see The Beatles!

When we got to the seventh floor, the door opened and there was no one at the concierge podium to greet us. All the people in the restaurant, including waiters, waitresses, the concierge, cooks, etc., were up to the windows to see The Beatles come in. As Mike and I joined the "Window

Gang," an announcement was made that The Beatles plane had just landed. We saw the plane taxi in. Then the door opened and four - two inch tall musicians stepped out of the plane. We were up so high, that everything on the ground looked like toys. We only knew it was The Beatles because of the deafening sound made by 7,000 screaming fans when they came out of the plane.

After disembarking from the plane, The Beatles were taken in a three-limousine convoy to their hotel. We watched them get in the middle limo. As the three limousines started to leave the airfield, they went under a terminal four-way tunnel bridge. The first limo went straight out to where mobs of teenagers were waiting. The second limo, with The Beatles in it, took a right turn and went out to a back dirt road, to escape the mob. The third limo went straight, pretending to be "The Beatles" limo, and got mobbed. They had to stop. The limo could not move without running someone over. The crowd finally dissipated when they realized The Beatles were not in the limo. Because of where Mike and I were, we saw the whole thing.

Phil, on the other hand, had managed to get on the terminal tunnel bridge. He saw John Lennon's hand waving out the back of the limo as it passed under him, with 6,000 screaming girls compressed against him. Wow! Lucky Phil. Bob however, got a close-up, "VIP view" of...... some Beatle Impersonators. They were on a baggage cart, riding around and waving to the crowd.

We finally re-grouped, exchanged stories of what we saw, and left. We didn't have any trouble leaving, because 7,000 fans were still there. They didn't realize that The Beatles were not at the airport anymore; they were sticking around.

When we got back, I cooked supper: steak, potatoes and corn. I then called Chick and told her all about The Beatles and the experiences we had. We then went over to Porky's to see if he had any one night jobs for us yet. He claimed that he had a three night job for $500.00, but had to let it go because he couldn't find us. Boy, were we upset!

We decided that since we had no other plans, and almost no money, that we would go to a drive in movie. We had seen a newspaper ad that said, "Cars with out-of-state license plates can get in free." We saw "The Days of Wine and Roses." We finally got home at 3:00 am. We were tired, but in good health.

February 14, 1964 (Friday)

We got up at 1:00 pm. Phil forgot to lock the Kingtones' van the night before. All of our equipment was in it. He then left the keys on someone else's car. What could have been a catastrophe, just turned out to be the "Absent Minded Professor." This was the start of Phil's new nickname, "Fog."

I cooked breakfast, and we finished eating at 2:40 pm. Once again, we went to Porky's to see if he had found us a one night job. The good news was that he had a "Valentine Party" for us to play. The bad news was that it only paid $60.00. Normally, we would have turned it down because of the low pay. But since we were almost out of money, and any money was better than none, we took the job.

We went over to the house where the party was to take place, and set the equipment up. We then left, went home, ate supper and went back to play. We started at 9:00 pm. The crowd really liked us. The louder we played the more wild they got. We finished playing at 1:45 am. I then went to get our money; I was told that Porky would be paying us, and we needed to see him in the morning.

I immediately started packing up. There was no need to socialize or flirt with the girls, because I had Chick waiting for me in Michigan. The other four guys, however, were "footloose and fancy free;" they were looking for some action. They mingled with the crowd, had a few drinks and tried to impress the girls with their "Rock Star" attitude. In the meantime, I was the only one packing up. I was tired and pissed. Whatever "bull" the boys were using to pick up the girls evidently wasn't working. Before long they were helping me. We finished packing and left around 4:00 am. We were still healthy and getting along okay.

February 15, 1964 (Saturday)

We got up about 11:30 am and ate breakfast. We decided to go to the beach for the day. Phil wanted to stay and relax at the apartment. He probably needed some time away from the rest of us. On our way to the beach, we stopped at Porky's and collected our $60.00 for last night's party. Porky said that he heard good things about us, and the crowd loved our music. We felt this probably confirmed Porky's decision to hire us. We left Porky's and finally got to the beach.

It was a beautiful day, with the temperature at 77 degrees. The sun was shining, and the water was warm. The only problem was that Fort Lauderdale, especially the beach area, was almost deserted. We walked around a little, and went into a few stores. Since there wasn't much happening, because it was not spring break yet, we went back to the apartment. I made dinner: rice, one hamburg a piece and stew. It was not the greatest supper, but it did curb our hunger.

After dinner, we met one of our neighbors in the apartment next to us. His name was Lloyd. He was in his mid-forties, very likeable and a great talker. He had a lot of self confidence, and made you believe he could do anything he set his mind too. We got along great, and he became a mentor to us.

We went to get a large pizza. The "fabulous dinner" that I made earlier was just not enough. We spent the rest of the night eating pizza and talking to Lloyd. Mike went to bed early, and Pete, as usual, went to the bar. We were getting along fair, but still in good health. I called Chick. I loved and missed her very much. I wanted to be back in Michigan with her.

February 16, 1964 (Sunday)

We got up about 10:15 am; Mike and I went to church. Pete, Bob and Phil slept in. When Mike and I returned, I fixed breakfast for everybody. Since it was another beautiful day, we all decided to go to the beach again. In spite of the fact that it was 82 degrees out, and very hot, we had a good time.

We returned in time for supper. The Beatles, once again, were going to be on television. This would be their second U.S. appearance on American TV. They were such a big hit the first time, Ed Sullivan brought them back. It was being telecast from Miami Beach. They were going to be on at 8:00 pm, with a second appearance to close the show. We had one small problem with this: we didn't have a television set. So we went knocking on Lloyd's door: our new best friend! He was delighted that we asked if we could watch The Beatles with him.

After the program was over, I went and called Chick. She told me that Cadet Distributing, our record company from Detroit had called, and our record *Twins*, was going to be released nationally. We were thrilled with the news! We started to wonder if we had made the right decision to come to Florida, instead of staying in Michigan to promote our record.

We were still healthy, but were getting on each other's nerves a lot. You could feel the tension, when we were all together. I was appointed to go out, over the next couple of days, to rent a television set. We hoped that a TV would help us occupy some of our time, when we had nothing to do. We also thought that maybe we wouldn't get on each other's nerves as much, if we got engrossed in some of the TV programs.

February 17, 1964 (Monday)

We got up at noon; Mike and I went downtown shopping. I didn't make breakfast, so we stopped at Burger King and got something to eat. Burger King was new to us; we didn't have any in Michigan. Bob and Phil went out and tried to get auditions for the band. They hoped that maybe they could get The Kingtones into a small club for a day or two. We needed the money. They were successful in getting two clubs to say that we could audition for them.

We decided to wash the van so that it would "shine" when we drove up for our auditions. We wanted to make a good first impression. I don't know if we used too much water or what, but our landlord came over and gave us heck for almost caving in the septic tanks.

Since it was such a beautiful day, I decided to go back to Fort Lauderdale. I wanted to go get a picture painted of me, to send to Chick. Mike and I had seen a place that painted portraits, when we were there earlier. Sorry to say, I wasted my money. The portrait was not very good. It could have been used by Pete, Bob, Mike or Phil as their portrait, and no one would have known the difference.

We ran out of peanut butter, so Mike went and bought some. He came back with a brand that we had never heard of. He was trying to save us money. We didn't notice any difference at first, but soon after eating it, everyone had the runs.

Pete, Phil and I were still in good health and Bob had a cold. We were not sure what was wrong with Mike, but he had a runny nose, dry cough and a high temperature. He was very sick. There was still a lot of tension in the air. We had not rented a television as of yet. Hopefully, we would do that tomorrow.

February 18, 1964 (Tuesday)

We got up about 9:00 am. We ate a quick breakfast, and headed out to audition for the two clubs that Phil and Bob stopped at yesterday. We arrived at the Peppermint Lounge, and asked where they would like us to set up for the audition. They said that they already had a band and to come back in two weeks. This was not good news. We needed a job NOW! Not in two weeks. We were hoping to be playing at Porky's in two weeks. We left there, and went to our second possibility: The Castaway. When we arrived, they told us that they were in a dispute with the Musicians' Union, and couldn't do anything with bands until it was settled: "Call back in a couple of days," they said. So what started out as Hope and Success, turned out to be *despair* and *failure*.

Since the two try-outs were not going to happen, I had several errands to run. I first went to the post office to mail the picture of me to Chick. I figured that even though it wasn't very good, she would probably still like it. My next stop was to take the "crappy" peanut butter back. They gave me a refund without any questions. The third, and most important errand, was to go rent a television set. I had called two TV rental places earlier, and got prices of $30.00 and $28.00 a month. As I started to drive to them, I saw a store that was real close to our apartment. It was advertising TV's for rent, so I stopped. They wanted $24.00 a month.... it was a done deal.

When I got back with the television, I was expecting a "Hero's Welcome..." "Let's hear it for Bruce; he got us a TV set, Yeah!" Instead, I got bitched at for paying too much for the rental. "How come you only got a 19 inch screen?" Bitch, complain, criticize, whine. I got mad! The apartment looked like a pigsty. I started yelling that I wanted the place cleaned up NOW! The boys knew I was mad, so reluctantly they helped clean it. We hooked up the TV, and as the boys became mesmerized by "the picture tube," I fixed supper.

We finally figured out what was wrong with Mike. He had the measles. His sister had them just before we left for Florida. Mike had never had them before, so now it was his turn. The four of us thought we had the measles when we were younger, but we were not sure. So we did our best to stay away from him. We thought about taking him to a doctor, or even the hospital, but since we were about broke, we just let the disease run its course.

My mother called me today. She said my Uncle Neil, who lived in

Florida, had passed away. She and my Dad were going to come to Florida for the funeral.

We were really low on money now. We had $22.00 left in the "kitty." We needed a job badly. Pete, Bob, Phil and I were basically still healthy. Mike, of course, was sick; tension was at an all time high.

February 19, 1964 (Wednesday)

I got up at 11 am. I was still upset about the way I was treated Tuesday night. I didn't feel that anyone appreciated all the things that I had been doing for them: cooking, cleaning, renting the TV, buying groceries, etc. So in retaliation, I put a new "rule" into effect: "Everyone had to make their own meal." The boys thought that was hilarious; they laughed and laughed. This made me even angrier. I had to get out of there before I said or did something that I would regret later. I left and went to Fort Lauderdale for the day. I also made a stop at the Mai Kai Restaurant and explored the grounds. It was one of the most beautiful landscaped properties I had ever seen.

When I returned, I fixed supper for Mike and me. I fixed Mike's because he was sick. Bob and Phil went and ate at Royal Castle. Pete ate Mike's leftovers. When Bob and Phil returned, Bob came in smoking a big cigar. I don't know if he was trying to be funny, or if he was trying to upset me even more. He knew I didn't care to have people smoke around me, and normally, Bob didn't smoke. Pete then jumped on this "festive moment," and started singing "Shake It up Jesus." This was followed by a good old discussion of sex. One of the boys said that he would screw any girl, any time, if she wanted it. This was followed by, "Don't worry; no one will ever want it from you!" You would have thought that this was the funniest thing anyone had ever said. They laughed and laughed.

I received two letters on that day: one from Chick and one from my mother. Getting Chick's letter helped me calm down inside. I really missed her. I felt that, at the present time, I was standing alone. Her letter made me feel better and made me realize that this frustrated state of mind would soon pass. I said a prayer asking God to take the anger out of me. After all, Bob, Pete, Phil and Mike, under normal circumstances, were my best friends.

The four boys appeared to be getting along okay. I needed to try a little attitude adjustment on myself, so that we could all get along better. Mike is still sick; the rest of us are "physically" healthy.

February 20, 1964 (Thursday)

We got up about 11:30 am. I made breakfast for Mike and me. Phil made pancakes for the rest of the boys. They, to my delight, didn't look very good. Pete and Bob said they looked like vomit; but they ate them.

The Kingtones van was broken down and Phil's car was also out of commission. Bob's car was our only mode of transportation at that time. Bob and Phil, once again went out to try and get us a job. They came back several hours later, unsuccessful.

Since we needed groceries, I took Bob's car and went to the store. I spent $15.00; this left $4.00 in our kitty. While I was gone, the boys cleaned up the apartment. They did a great job. I felt that they did this to help ease the tension that we all felt. Because of this, I decided to revoke my "cook your own meal rule" and started cooking for them again. At supper time, I cooked one of the best meals of the trip. When we finished, we went out to get some ice cream. We were having a great time and getting along just fine. I tried to analyze why we were getting along so well. Then it came to me: Pete was not with us. He was with our neighbor Lloyd, out drinking and trying to deal some girl.

Pete had a charismatic personality. He had a kind of inescapable magnetism that drew people to him. He often got people to do things that they normally might not do. Sometimes these things were so subtle, that you didn't even realize you were doing them: like making fun of someone and thinking it was cool. When Pete was not around, the four of us seemed to get along fine. When Pete came back into the picture, we started to have arguments, disagreements and began to quarrel. There seemed to be more tension in the air when he was around.

When we returned from the ice cream store, I called Chick. I missed her and it was great to hear her voice. We needed a job badly. We hoped that we would start at Porky's on Monday. Mike was looking and feeling much better. The rest of us were healthy. We were getting along well, while Pete, the "Puppet Master" was out.

February 21, 1964 (Friday)

We got up about noon. I fixed breakfast, and we all went to the beach except Phil. He wanted to stay and work on his car. It was a beautiful day and the sun was shining.

We walked the beach for a little while, but since it was basically void of people, we soon left and went to a pawn shop. I bought a $1.00 ring, Major bought a gun that shot blanks, and Pete purchased a harmonica. We returned to the apartment, ate supper and went to a movie.

After the movie, we stopped back at Porky's. When we got there, Porky gave us some disturbing news. The Musicians' Union was bitching about The Kingtones coming into Porky's without using a booking agent and without having a contract. The Musicians' Union was threatening Porky, telling him if he let us come in, they would not allow any other Union bands to play at his club. Since almost all bands at that time belonged to the Musicians' Union, that meant that Porky would not be able to have music at his club. Although The Kingtones did belong to the Musicians' Union, we didn't have a booking agent or a contract to play at Porky's. We were just sick about the news. It seemed like nothing was going our way.

Pete and I had a few words that day. I asked him why was it that whenever he was gone, we got along just fine, but when he was present, we seemed to have "dissention amongst the ranks." He said it was because he was cool and sophisticated and that I was uncool and dull. I was not sure that he answered my question, but I left it at that.

I missed Chick very much, and hoped that I would be seeing her soon; I didn't realize at the time I would see her sooner than I expected. Mike appeared to be better. We were all healthy.

February 22, 1964 (Saturday)

We woke up to the "beautiful" singing of Phil. He was trying to write a new song for our record company: a follow up to *The Girl I Love*. I got up and made breakfast. It was raining outside. The forecast was for rain and cloud cover the entire day.

Even though we were about out of money and had no job, our spirits were often lifted when we saw the sun. Today there was nothing going for us. We sat around and watched TV the rest of the morning and afternoon.

Phil finally suggested that we bring in the organ, and have a small "combo practice." He wanted to learn some more Beatles' tunes. This helped break up our monotonous day and we learned three new Beatles' songs.

At 6:30, I made supper. When we finished, we started to watch television again. Lloyd stopped over. Pete had told him of our troubles with the Musicians' Union and he had a possible solution for us. He suggested that we should get a Union Contract and back date it. Then we should take it to the Musicians' Union in Miami, for them to have on file. We were to say that we had sent Porky a contract in January, which he signed. Porky misplaced his copy of the contract, and therefore wasn't able to send it to the Musicians' Union ahead of time. We were coming to give them our copy to put on file. We thought if Porky would go along with this plan, it would work.

Our spirits were lifted up, and we had renewed hope. We were going to call Clyde Falk, the president of the Grand Rapids Musicians' Union, and ask him to send us a union contract. We would do it first thing in the morning.

We did not get along as well today as yesterday, but it was tolerable. All of us were healthy, but very sick of sitting around doing nothing. We only had $4.00 left in the kitty, and we were in need of food.

February 23, 1964 (Sunday)

I set my alarm, so I could get up and go to church. It was a rather chilly day outside, but the sun was out. I was going to walk to church today, because The Kingtones' van was broke and Phil's car was also out of commission; Major would not let me take his car. Fortunately, the church was only a half mile down the road.

After I left church, I stopped and bought a few groceries. When I got back to the apartment, I made breakfast. The boys were watching television. We had no plans that day, and since it was cool out, we weren't going to the beach. This turned out to be a "TV Day"! TV in the morning, TV in the afternoon, and TV at supper time. For dinner, I prepared a delicious meal of hot dogs and beans.

My mother and dad had come to Florida to go to my Uncle Neil's Funeral. They stopped by our apartment, and offered to take us out for pizza. We had just finished eating, and we were not hungry. But "Hey!" you just don't turn down free food. So we got a break from the TV set, and went to have some pizza. They bought us two large pizzas. When we had finished eating, we were all stuffed and felt kind of sick. As my folks got ready to leave, I was feeling very sad; I didn't want them to go. My mother could sense my sadness and decided to cheer me up with a little surprise. She said that in two weeks she and my father were going to return to Florida and bring my sister Lorraine and Chick with them. I couldn't believe my ears! She was going to bring Chick!! I was so excited, I couldn't stand it! I wanted to call her! I missed her so much and couldn't wait until she arrived!

When we returned to the apartment, you could never have guessed what we decided to do. That's right! We watched more TV! Yahoo TV! We were all healthy and getting along fairly well.

February 24, 1964 (Monday)

We woke up during the middle of the night because our water heater blew up. There was water all over the floor. We quickly shut the water off, mopped up the floor, and went back to bed. We got up at 12:30 pm. I made pancakes for breakfast, without any eggs. I had to use our electric frying pan, because our stove was broken. After breakfast, we went and told the landlord that we had no gas to cook with and no hot water to wash with. He came over and fixed them both.

We were waiting anxiously for the mailman to come. We had called the Grand Rapids Musicians' Union, and they were going to send us union contracts immediately. We were hoping that we would get them that day. The union contracts did arrive that day, along with two letters from Chick. I was more thrilled receiving two letters from Chick, than I was about getting the union contracts.

It was another beautiful day outside, with the sun shining and the temperature at 75 degrees. We went to Porky's to talk to him about our plan. If he liked the idea, and was willing to go along with it, we would give him the union contracts to sign.

When we got there, Porky was talking to some band from Indiana. They were going to start playing that night, because he didn't dare start us yet. He was afraid of the union sanctions that might be placed on his club, if he let us play. We told him of our plan and showed him the union contract. He liked the idea and told us to come back Wednesday, and we would discuss our pay and the hours we would be playing. He said that we could probably start in a week. We told him that we wanted to know on Wednesday if we were going to start for sure by March 2. If we were not starting by then, we were packing up and going back to Michigan.

We left Porky's and returned to our apartment. I made supper. I liked to experiment with different foods, from time to time, to help break up the monotony of cooking. On this night, we were going to have corned beef hash, mixed with tomato soup. I have to admit, it didn't look very good, but it actually tasted okay. After dinner, we watched TV. I tried to call Chick, but her mother said she had gone roller skating. I sure missed her. We finally decided that we couldn't stand TV anymore; so we went to the movies.

After the movie, we went back to Porky's. We wanted to hear what our competition sounded like. They were a decent band, but we felt that we were much better. We were all healthy, but still not getting along very well. We had way too much time on our hands, and continued to get on each others' nerves.

February 25, 1964 (Tuesday)

We got up at 11:30 am. I made breakfast of cheese sandwiches. We were out of "official" breakfast food. It was another nice day: warm with low humidity. I received a letter from Chick, so I called her. I really wanted to hear her voice. When she answered, I spent the next 8 minutes in "Heaven." I forgot all the problems I was having in Florida, and concentrated on the happy, fun loving thoughts of her.

The rest of the day was a hodgepodge of not doing much. We played some cards, and of course, watched more television: our all time favorite thing to do. I went to the cleaners and picked up our band suits. We wanted to be ready if we started at Porky's on Monday. We had an optimistic outlook about our chances of playing there. We had seen an ad in the newspaper which said The Kingtones would be starting at Porky's March 2.

We took a little break from TV, to listen to the World's Heavyweight Boxing Championship on the radio. If it was televised, we couldn't get it. The fight was between Sonny Liston and Cassius Clay. Pete bet me a dime that Cassius Clay would win. Normally, I wouldn't take a bet, but I thought I would teach Pete a good lesson about betting. I knew that Sonny had beat Floyd Patterson in the first round with a knockout. All the odds makers were saying that Liston would "cream" Clay. So I took his dime bet, and prepared a mental speech of how he was a fool to bet. Of course, when the fight was over, and Cassius Clay won, this just confirmed Pete that HE too "Was the Greatest." He also let me know that I was a loser! After the fight, I made popcorn. We quickly resumed our "television positions," and watched TV until every channel had gone off the air.

Pete had mentioned earlier, that if we wanted to, we could get a job at the Shelazar Bar for $25.00 a night. We decided that if we didn't start at Porky's on March 2, we would play there for 3 or 4 nights. That way, we would have enough money for gas and food on our trip back to Michigan.

We were all healthy and got along very well that day. That was the first time in ages that we didn't have disagreements. One of the reasons that our day might have gone so well was because Pete was out of money, except for 16 cents. He hadn't had a beer all day and even got the shakes. His mind was on other things than finding fault with us.

February 26, 1964 (Wednesday)

We got up about 1:30 pm. I fixed breakfast: baloney sandwiches. We were still out of "breakfast food." It was a warm day with a beautiful blue sky. We went to Porky's to discuss our pay, and the hours we would work. We wanted to get the contract signed, so that we could take it to the Musicians' Union as soon as possible.

Porky started off our "negotiations" by saying that he never paid union scale. He was going to make the contract out for $650.00, union minimum pay, but he was going to pay us only $475.00 a week. The hours we would be working were 9:30 pm to 3:30 am. On the contract, however, he was going to put 10:00 pm to 3:00 am. We would be playing six nights a week, Wednesday thru Monday, with Tuesday being our day off. During Spring Break, he would be running two bands. We would play a half hour, and then band two would come on stage and play for half an hour. We would continue alternating every half hour, until 3:30 am. He wanted us to share equipment, as much as possible, like one drum set on stage. He didn't want the music to ever stop, because of us having to set up or tear down. During spring break, he was also going to run some afternoon jam sessions. He said he would let us know more about that later. He told us he would fill out the contract, and we could pick it up on Friday.

We left the contract with Porky and went back to our apartment. We were not happy about the low pay and the long hours. On the bright side, however, he was paying us more than what Captain Joe was going to pay us. Then too, Porky's was the second hottest night club, soon to be number one, in Fort Lauderdale. We felt that the exposure, experience and prestige from playing there would certainly help us get more jobs and better pay in the future.

When we got back, Mike, Pete, Bob and I played poker with match sticks. Phil had a headache from trying to negotiate with Porky, and went to sleep on the coach. I fixed supper around 7:30 pm. It actually turned out to be a very good dinner, considering how low on food we were. We had American fries, peas, fried baloney, fried onions, bread and Kool-aid.

After dinner, the four card players continued playing until 12:30 am. We then decided to go back to Porky's to see Billy & Lillie and the Thunderbirds. This was a special lounge act that Porky had brought in from Las Vegas. They were only going to be at Porky's for just three weeks. They were excellent! But they definitely were not a rock 'n roll band. If we started at Porky's on March 2, like we hoped we would, we would be alternating sets with them. We were all still healthy, and got along very well that day.

February 27, 1964 (Thursday)

We got up at 2:30 pm. I made breakfast of peanut butter and jelly sandwiches. We had enough food left for about three more meals; we had 22 cents left in the kitty. I called home and talked to my brother Chuck. It was nice hearing his voice. I then called Chick; it was always great talking to her!

Lloyd had a friend that managed a bar called The Banion Club. He told us that he had arranged an audition with his friend at the Shelazar Bar. He knew we were probably going to Porky's on March 2. But he said that if something should happen that we didn't go in, this might be a place we could play. After all, we would need to earn some money to get back home. So we went over to the Shelazar Bar, set up our equipment and played for an hour.

We never saw Lloyd's friend, but Lloyd claimed he was there. We didn't make a big deal out of it, since we figured we were going into Porky's anyway. Besides, we had no other plans for that day, and it gave us a chance to try out the acoustics in the Shelazar, in case we needed to play there for gas money back to Michigan. We also knew that Lloyd often stretched the truth a little bit. But he had been a good neighbor, and we didn't want to strain our relationship with him.

We packed up and went back to our apartment around 5:20 pm; I cooked supper. Once again we watched TV for our evening's entertainment. I decided, around 12:45 am, out of boredom, to practice my organ. Phil couldn't hear the TV very well, because of my organ playing, and turned it up. Then I couldn't hear my organ very well, so I turned IT up. It became a duel! Who could be heard, him or me? At 1:10 am, there was a knock on our door. It was the landlord. He told us to turn the organ off and the TV way down! He was not a happy camper! We didn't get along very well that day; we had several quarrels.

February 28, 1964 (Friday)

We didn't get to sleep until 5:30 am. We started to reminisce about our past: old girl friends, participation in sports, singing on "Aunt Bertha's Bible Hour," vacations, etc. We set our alarm to wake us up at 12:15 pm. We were going to go pick up our Union Contract from Porky, and take it to the Musicians' Union in Miami. We wanted to make sure they got it before we started playing at Porky's on Monday, March 2.

Mike and I crawled out of bed at the sound of the alarm. Phil, Bob and Pete refused to get up. Bob said we could take his car to go to Porky's. After we picked up the contract, he wanted us to return to the apartment to get Phil and him. Pete didn't want to go.

Mike and I went and picked up the contract. As we looked it over, we wished that Phil would have come with us. He knew a lot more about contracts then we did. It seemed to us that the contract was very evasive. Where it said, "Name and Address of Place of Employment," there was one word – PORKY'S. "Hours of Employment," 10 to 3, along with a pen scratching note that said, "2 week written notice on either part to terminate contract." That made us a little nervous. Then too, Porky put the "number of musicians" in the band at 4. We figured he must have done that, because even at minimum wage, $650.00 was probably for four musicians, not five. What we did like was it looked like Porky signed the contract on January 24, 1964. He also included a small message indicating he had sent us $75.00 in advance for "Travel Money." We hoped the Musicians' Union would accept the contract.

We returned to the apartment and got Phil and Bob. Just as we were about to leave, Lloyd came over. He told us that he had just got a job managing a motel in Miami; he would be leaving on Sunday. He said he would let us know the phone number and address of the motel, once he moved in. He invited us to come and see him and swim in the pool. We figured this was another one of Lloyd's "Bull Stories." We told him that once he got settled, to let us know and we would come and visit him.

It was a very hot afternoon: 84 degrees. Bob drove and we left for Miami. When we got to the Musicians' Union, we didn't know exactly where the office was. We found this huge building with a sign on it that said, "American Federation of Musicians – Local 655," so we entered the first door we came to. When we got inside, the room looked like a gym. All over the gym were unemployed musicians just waiting for the phone to ring. They were hoping that someone would call and say, "I need a guitar player for tonight, or sax player, drummer, a trumpet player," etc. We asked where the office was so we could file our contract. It seemed like every eye in the place was then staring at us with hate on their face. We felt very bad about all the unemployed musicians, but we needed to work also.

When we entered the office, I was the one that was designated to do all the talking. I even signed the contract, like I was the leader. Although Phil was the leader, he was not a very good liar; I could lie with the best of them. I told them the story of how I contacted Porky back in January to play at his club and sent him contracts. He signed them and sent me my copy, along with $75.00 in advance for travel money. He was supposed to send a copy of the contract to the Musicians' Union, but he misplaced it. We, therefore, had come down to bring them our copy to have on file. The man behind the desk took our contract, made a copy of it and said that he hoped we would enjoy playing at Porky's. That was it! No questions! No lectures! He did say, however, to make sure we paid our Union Work Dues on time. We left and returned to our apartment.

When we got back, I made supper. We had almost no food left and there was no money in the kitty. The kitty actually owed us money. After dinner, we watched more TV. Since there was nothing good on, the boys decided to play cards. I wrote Chick a letter; I missed her so much. I said a long prayer and went to sleep. I woke up in the middle of the night almost frozen. I couldn't believe how cold it was: From 84 degrees to what felt like 34 degrees. What crazy weather. We were all healthy and got along well that day.

February 29, 1964 (Saturday)

I got up at 11:30 am. I made breakfast, loosely speaking. I had so little food that I decided to make a spaghetti casserole. I took spaghetti, chicken noodle soup, tuna and onions and mixed them all together. I baked them for half an hour. When it was finished, and the boys sampled it, the "breakfast" was declared the worst meal that they ever had! They wouldn't eat it. They said they would rather starve!

As usual, the boys took their TV positions and started their television marathon. It was a beautiful day outside, but I couldn't take advantage of it except to go for a walk. The only working vehicle was Bob's. He didn't want to do anything except watch TV and he wouldn't let me take his car. I don't know how he could stand that much TV, it was driving me crazy! I got a letter from Chick, however, which helped me keep my sanity for a little while.

At supper time, I decided to try a vegetable stew. I mixed mashed potatoes with creamed corn, regular corn, peas and carrots and chicken noodle soup and cooked them. What a mess! This now became the number one worst meal the boys ever had. Once again, they refused to eat it.

My "special breakfast," along with my "unique dinner," did have a positive effect on getting the boys away from the TV and out of the apartment. They held out, however, until 2 am. By then they were so hungry that we all went to Royal Castle for something to eat!

When we finished eating, we went to the Friendly Bull Bar. They had a famous organ player performing there, that we wanted to see. He was excellent, but we were so tired by then, we couldn't really appreciate him. We didn't stay long; we went back to our apartment and went to bed.

The boys were basically healthy. I was worried about a pain in my back along with a small spot on my chest which seemed to bleed quite often. I thought if it continued to bleed, I would go see a doctor.

March 1, 1964 (Sunday)

We got up at 2 pm. I didn't make it to church that day; I was just too tired. Mike decided to make breakfast for us. He figured that he couldn't do any worse than my "spaghetti casserole". He made chop suey. It was almost as bad as my breakfast. The big difference was that the boys ate a little bit of it, even though they complained. After breakfast, the boys immediately took up their TV positions and turned on the "boob tube." I suggested that we work on some new songs for Porky's, but nobody answered; they were already in a trance and didn't want to practice.

I was pissed, so I decided to go and look for a place for my family and Chick to stay while they were here. I wanted them to stay close to our apartment, so I could spend more time with her. It was a very hot and humid day. It was not the best time of day to be checking on motels. I tried three motels and one apartment complex, to see if they had any rooms available during the time my folks would be here; I didn't have any luck. I figured I would try again tomorrow.

When I got back to our apartment, no one had moved. They were still watching TV. I thought, "What a bunch of lazy asses." I then suggested that we go to the Dairy Queen. Phil was the only one who responded. He and I walked there; I got a large ice cream cone and Phil got a hot fudge sundae. I poured out my frustration to him: the boys always watching TV, never wanting to do anything else and never helping with the household chores. Phil assured me that this was just a phase they were going through and it would not last.

When we got back, I started to clean the apartment. I even washed the floors. Phil joined in and so did Mike. Pete even picked up a little bit, but Major didn't move a muscle. Hence, the nickname "Bob the Blob" was created. I was so mad at Bob for not helping, that I said I wasn't going to make supper. Instead I made popcorn. The smell of the popcorn made everybody hungry. I refused to give any of MY popcorn to Bob or Pete; Mike and Phil were welcome to have some. Pete and Bob were very mad that I wouldn't give them any popcorn. They took off, along with Mike, to go get something to eat.

I tried to call Chick two different times that night. I really wanted to hear her friendly, loving voice. Sorry to say, the lines were all tied up and I couldn't get through. Phil, Mike and I were getting along well. Bob and Pete were getting along fine with each other, but not with me. Once again there was a lot of tension in the air.

March 2, 1964 (Monday)

We got up at 10 am; what a miracle. I fixed TV dinners for breakfast, since that was the only food left in the apartment. We went to Porky's to set up. When we got there, we noticed the stage was in the shape of a horseshoe. It was approximately 42 inches high. The Kingtones liked a rectangular stage that was about eight inches off the floor. In front of the stage were the bartenders, with the bar in front of them; we got to see their backs all night. The dance floor was in the shape of the number seven. As we looked out at our audience from the stage, a short narrow dance floor was in front of the bar. On the right side of the bar was a much larger dance floor, which connected to the dance floor in front. Attached to the back of the stage was a dressing room for the band. We could change there and even spend our breaks there, if we didn't want to socialize. We finally got set up and practiced for awhile. After a couple of hours, we took a break. During that time, we took The Kingtones' van to the Ford dealer to get fixed. Major followed us in his car, so we would have a way back to Porky's. We dropped the van off; returned to Porky's and practiced for another hour.

We finally left and went back to our apartment. Since we didn't have any food, we went out for supper. When we finished, we went back home and got dressed in our band uniforms. We watched a little TV and tried to get ourselves mentally ready for the long six hour night.

We left for Porky's around 8:30 pm. Even though Porky's was only about a half hour away, we wanted to make sure we were not late, especially on our first night. We started playing at 9:30 pm. We had a lot of adjustments to make with our equipment and the stage. When we started, about 1/3 of the place was filled; the "Spring Breakers" had not started coming yet. After about an hour of turning our volume down, then turning it up, moving the equipment closer to the back wall, then moving it away from the wall, we started to get in the groove. While we were trying to get our sound right, we were also battling the hired help. They kept telling us what to do.

We finally got a good sound and had three excellent sets. We held our crowd, although small, until 2:30 am. At that time, most of the customers cleared out. Because of the small crowd and the band being exhausted, our last set was not very good. Of course this happened to be the time that Porky showed up. He came in to see six people in the audience and a band that wasn't performing up to par. He complained a bit, but after looking at the cash register receipts, he didn't say any more.

During the night, every time we took a break, we made Mike stay in the dressing room behind the stage. Although he appeared to be healthy, he still had a slight rash from the measles. We did not want to take any chance of Mike passing on the measles' germs, if he was still contagious.

When we got back to our apartment, it was 4:30 am. There was a message for us from our recording company to call Detroit. Phil said he would call them when he got up. The temperature that day had been a little warm, but it was still a very nice day. The boys were all healthy and getting along okay. We were absolutely exhausted.

March 3, 1964 (Tuesday)

We got up at noon. We just couldn't sleep; it was too hot! The temperature was already in the 80s and it was supposed to get up to the 90s by midday. Phil called our record company in Detroit to see what they wanted. They just wanted to tell us that our record "Twins," was still number 17 in Detroit for the second week in a row. They also re-emphasized that they were in the process of releasing *Twins* nationally. That was great news!

Now that we were working at Porky's, Phil said he would loan the kitty $50.00 so we could buy some food. Mike, Phil and I all went to the store. We loaded up on cereal, canned goods, boxed food items, potatoes, TV dinners, bread, Kool-Aid, etc. We spent $38.98. We hoped that this would last us for at least a couple of weeks.

Since Tuesday was our day off from playing at Porky's, we decided to go to the beach. We hadn't been there more than fifteen minutes when Mike (a.k.a. Clod) stepped on a jellyfish. We didn't know what was going on at first, but Mike started yelling and dropped to the sand to examine his foot. He pointed to a small jellyfish that had washed up on the shore. We had heard that salt was a good thing to put on a jellyfish sting, so we had Mike put his foot in the Atlantic Ocean. That was the only salt we had; it actually helped to reduce the pain. Phil went and bought some Benadryl cream which he said would stop the itching and help relieve the pain. That ended our great day at the beach.

We returned to the apartment, where I made a wonderful dinner: steak, mashed potatoes, green beans, grape & banana fruit salad, fried onions and of course good old Kool-Aid. The boys loved it. Everybody ate like it was their last meal. We were so full, we could hardly move. Phil, however, claimed that he wasn't that full. I bet him a dime that he couldn't eat four more pieces of bread with jelly on them. Phil, not wanting to lose face, took my bet. The good news – Phil won the bet; the bad news - he lay on the bed groaning for hours.

I called home and talked to my mother. I wanted to know when she thought they would arrive in Fort Lauderdale. She said they would be leaving Grand Rapids on March 5 and hoped to be to our place on March 7. I just couldn't wait to see Chick! We watched TV the rest of the night. What a surprise! We got along better today than yesterday, but not as good as we should have. All of us were healthy, if you can call recovering from the measles and nursing a jellyfish sting healthy! Otherwise, four of us were healthy.

March 4, 1964 (Wednesday)

We got up at 12:30 pm. It was a little cooler outside that day: only 81 degrees. We ate breakfast and went to Porky's. He wanted us to rehearse. When we got there, we were told that we had just missed him. We practiced for some time and then took a break. We thought Porky wanted to be there to hear us practice, so we waited for a while. Since he didn't come, we practiced some more and then took another break. We were there until 5:00 pm; Porky never showed. We finally called it quits and went back to our apartment.

When we got back, I went out and tried to find a motel for my family and Chick; I still didn't have any luck. I figured I would try again the next day. I returned to our place where the boys.... you guessed it, were watching television. I fixed supper; we got ready and went back to Porky's.

When we got to the club, Porky wanted to know why we were late for practice that afternoon. We told him we didn't realize we were supposed to be there at a specific time. He said if it happened again, he might have to dock our pay. We WANTED to say, "You don't pay us to practice, so how can you dock us?" But we were looking at a 350 pound, gangster looking man, so we didn't say anything. Gee, Porky seemed to be so nice in the beginning, but now acted like an evil dictator.

We started playing that night at 9:27 pm; we didn't want to give Porky anything to gripe about. The crowd was a little bigger than on Monday. We had six very good sets. We kept 90 percent of our crowd until 2:30 am. That last hour was a killer, for the band as well as the audience. We felt that we held our crowd better than Billy & Lilly and we knew Porky paid them more than $78.00 a night. When we finished playing and got ready to leave, Porky smiled and said, "Good job, see you tomorrow night." We couldn't believe it, a compliment from Porky! We went back to our apartment very tired. I made myself a snack and went to bed. We were all healthy and got along alright that day.

March 5, 1964 (Thursday)

I got up at 9 am to watch a TV special on the late Al Jolson. We actually thought that we might do an impersonation of him. We were influenced by the Thunderbirds. Because I didn't get to bed until around 4:30 am, I kept falling asleep during the program. I finally shut the TV off and went back to bed. I had hardly gotten to sleep, when a tree cutter started up his chain saw to cut down limbs. It was not a very restful night. We never talked about Al Jolson again.

I finally got up and made breakfast. As the boys took their TV positions, I went out looking for a motel for my parents and Chick to stay at when they got there. It was 87 degrees out: very hot! This quest for a motel was becoming a nightmare. I could not find a room available. As I trudged down the road back to our place, I spotted an apartment with a "For Rent" sign on the office door. I stopped to see if they would rent me an apartment for one week. Normally they rented by the month, but since they had several apartments vacant, they said they would rent me one for a week. Hallelujah, my nightmare was over. When I got back, I was really tired. I did not want to make supper, but if I didn't make it, we wouldn't eat; I made spaghetti.

We left for Porky's at 8:45 pm. It was a different kind of night. We made a lot of musical mistakes: wrong chord here, wrong note there, not ending the song at the same time, etc. Pete, who was usually a master at calling the right songs at the right time, had an "off night." No matter what song he called, it wasn't the one he should have called. In spite of all our mistakes, our overall sound was good and we held the crowd. It seemed like the hours just dragged; it was a long night.

When we finished and got ready to leave, Pete told us to go on without him. He had met some girl and was going to try and deal her. It was a rather cool night outside, but Pete was willing to hitchhike home in the name of "love." We all laughed, called him "sucker," and left. We were all healthy; Mike's measles rash had cleared up and we were getting along well. The six hour sets were getting to us; we were getting sick of playing.

March 6, 1964 (Friday)

We got up at 2:30 pm. It was a beautiful day outside and the temperature was 75 degrees. I fixed breakfast half-heartedly; I was getting sick of cooking. We decided that we needed to make out a list of the songs we wanted to do each set. We also wanted to put them in the order they would be played. We worked on it most of the day. We finished the list around 8:00 pm; I then fixed supper. By the time dinner was done and we finished eating, we didn't have much time left to get to Porky's. We left the apartment at 9:05 pm and got to Porky's just in time to walk on the stage and start playing.

It was not a good night. During our first set, Phil's amp stopped working. He had blown a tube and didn't have a spare. There was another amp on the stage from the Thunderbirds that Phil did use, but it was totally different in sound than what we were use to; it didn't "rock." To make matters worse, Pete, the boy with the "stainless steel vocal cords," went hoarse. He stopped singing in the middle of a song and left the stage. What a nightmare! Needless to say, we did not sound very good; we went through six sets of hell! At the end of the night, Porky said that we were the worst sounding show band he ever saw. We were so frustrated and upset that we really didn't care if Porky fired us.

By the time we got back to our apartment, we were laughing about all the rotten things that happened to us; we were very tired. Everyone was physically healthy and we were getting along okay. Chick was coming in sometime later that day, and I couldn't wait to see her.

March 7, 1964 (Saturday)

We got up at 12:30 pm. It was a very hot day: 87 degrees. Phil and I went looking for tubes for his amp. After about an hour's search, we found what he needed. I made sure he bought a couple of extra ones.

We returned to our apartment and picked up Bob and Mike. Phil wanted to practice at Porky's. He was not happy with our sound and wanted to try some different things to make it better. Pete had taken off earlier and hitch-hiked to the beach, so naturally he wouldn't be there for practice. Mike said that my mother had called while we were gone and they would be to our place around 7 pm.

When we got to Porky's, Phil started working on our sound. First he tried turning the guitar and bass speakers backwards: closer to the wall, then away from the wall. He turned the guitar speakers upside down. He was trying everything he could think of. Since most of our songs had vocals in them, it was a little difficult to find a good sound without Pete. We finally quit, without much success and returned to our apartment. When we got back I made supper: hamburgs and pork & beans.

After eating, I asked the boys to help me pick up and clean the apartment a little, so my parents wouldn't think we were slobs. Surprisingly, everyone pitched in and helped: even Bob. In forty-five minutes the place looked respectable.

At 7:15 pm, Chick arrived. I was so excited I couldn't stand it! Because my parents and sister were with her, I had to hold back on my desire to give her a long passionate kiss and hug her to pieces. I greeted everyone, gave Chick a small kiss and hug and then showed them our apartment. After the apartment's "Grand Tour," I took them to their apartment that I had rented for them two days earlier. My folks were impressed. It had a full kitchen, living room, two bedrooms and two bathrooms. They were use to a small motel room. I stayed with them until I had to go play at Porky's. As excited as Chick was to see me, she was very tired and thought it would be best to stay with my folks and go to Porky's with me on Sunday.

I don't remember a lot about our playing on March 7; my mind was totally on Chick. I do remember that we just could not get a good sound. No matter what Phil tried, it didn't work, at least to his satisfaction. I thought he might start cracking up if he didn't figure out something soon. We were all healthy and were getting along okay.

March 8, 1964 (Sunday)

I got up at 10 am. My family and Chick came over and picked me up; I spent the day with them and had a great time. My mom and dad bought me breakfast, lunch and dinner. We went sightseeing and shopping. As long as I was with Chick, I didn't care what we did.

Meanwhile back at the Kingtones' apartment, everyone got up around 2:00 pm. The boys had to fix their own breakfast/lunch. Since Mike and I were the only two that would cook, cereal and peanut butter & jelly became their meals of choice. After they finished eating, Mike and Phil decided that it was time to wash some clothes; they spent the next two hours at the Laundromat. The rest of the day was spent watching TV. Pete, of course, spent most of his day at the Shelazar Bar.

I got back around 7:30 pm to get ready to go to Porky's. Because Chick was only 18, and I hadn't asked Porky if she could come in yet, she did not go with us. We got to the club at 9:00 pm. I immediately went and asked Porky if I could bring Chick into the club the next couple of nights. I wanted to ask him before we went on stage and played, in case we sounded bad. He said that as long as she didn't drink alcohol, he did not have a problem with it.

Once again we were having trouble finding the "Kingtones' Sound". There were a few songs that sounded like we were starting to get in the groove with them, but they were in the minority. We sounded a little better that night than we had on Saturday, but Phil was still not happy.

When we finished, Porky paid us half of our wages. He said he would pay us the rest on Monday night. We left and went back to our apartment. We were all discouraged about our sound. In fact, we were not very happy with most of our Florida experiences so far; our morale was low. Upon arriving at our apartment, we discovered that we had locked ourselves out. This was just one more problem to increase our frustration. Pete was so pissed; he broke the screen in the door to get in. We were all healthy, but we were starting to get on each other's nerves again, mostly because of our sound problems at Porky's.

March 9, 1964 (Monday)

I got up at 11 o'clock and walked over to Chick's apartment. They were getting ready to go to lunch, so I joined them. It was a very hot day outside, in spite of the sky being overcast. After lunch, Chick and I went to the Kingtones' apartment. Phil, Mike and Bob were just going to the beach to cool off, so we joined them. Pete, as usual, didn't want to go.

When we got to the beach, it started to rain. We were so mad; we lay out on the beach anyway. Since the rain was persistent and started coming down harder, we finally gave in and went shopping. We then returned to our apartment where Chick and I made supper.

The boys left for Porky's at 8:30 pm. Chick and I rode with my folks and sister; we followed Bob's car. That night was going to be a "killer," because The Thunderbirds had the night off and we had to play six forty minute sets.

Before we started, a girl came up to us and asked if we had a record out called *Twins*. She said she was from Toledo and the radio stations there were playing it. This lifted our spirits; we felt proud, excited, happy and important. She asked us for our autographs.

With a renewed frame of mind, we took to the stage. We also didn't have to worry about The Thunderbirds changing the mood and atmosphere from rock to pop, rhythm & Blues. With Phil at the helm, controlling the volume and sound and Pete singing his best to impress some girls sitting at a table nearby, we started to get the "Kingtones' Sound." We were good! The audience loved us. It was a long night, but we enjoyed playing for the first time in a long time. I was especially happy because my family and Chick were there and we were sounding great.

Porky paid us the rest of the money he owed us, and told us we did a great job. The girls that Pete had been trying to impress with his singing left just before we finished playing for the night; we just laughed.

We got home at 4:30 am. We were very tired, but had a much more positive outlook on our sound and playing. We were all healthy and got along well that day.

March 10, 1964 (Tuesday)

I got up at 10:30 am. I was so tired I could hardly open my eyes. Chick and I were going to spend the day and evening together by ourselves. The Kingtones did not have to play at Porky's on Tuesday; that was our night off. I called several car rental agencies to see how much I could rent a car for; because I was under 25 years old, I was told I would have to pay an extra fee. Bob, always "trying to be helpful," said I could rent his car for whatever the car rental agency would charge me, without the extra fee; I rented Bob's car.

It was another hot day, so Chick and I went to the beach. We ate all three meals out and went shopping. Meanwhile back at the Kingtones' apartment, the boys got up at 2:30 pm; cereal or peanut butter & jelly continued to be their meals of choice. After breakfast/lunch, Bob, Phil and Mike took Phil's car to the Ford dealer, picked up The Kingtones' van and left Phil's car there to get it fixed. Pete didn't want to go. The van cost us $168.00 for the repairs. The boys then returned to the apartment for another day and night "TV Marathon." We were all healthy and getting along satisfactory.

March 11, 1964 (Wednesday)

I got up at 10:30 am. Chick had invited me over to my folk's apartment for breakfast, and I was looking forward to having her cook for me. This was her last day in Florida; they were leaving for Michigan on Thursday morning. I spent some time with my family and then took Chick for a walk. I became the "tour guide," showing her Pete's second home, the Shelazar Bar, our favorite grocery store, the Dairy Queen and other "attractions" in the area. We had a great time, just walking, talking and holding hands.

Meanwhile back at our apartment, the boys tried, on three different occasions, to use the Kingtones' van to run some errands. Each time they had to push it with Major's car and pop the clutch to get it started. Evidently, the Ford Dealer that fixed the van overlooked the need for a new starter. Phil was going to take it back to the dealership in the morning.

It was another very hot day, so Chick and I stopped back at the Kingtones' apartment to see if anyone wanted to go to the beach. Bob, Mike and Phil wanted to go. Pete preferred to go to the air conditioned Shelazar Bar. When we got to the beach, everybody put on suntan lotion and lay out in the sun. After a half hour, someone mentioned how red we were getting. Sure enough, we were all sunburned except Chick. Of the four boys, Bob was burned the worst; Mike and Phil tied for second place and I was burned the least. We quickly put on our t-shirts and returned to our apartment to stay out of the sun. On our way back, we stopped at a drug store and bought some MediQuick First Aid Spray. This was supposed to take the pain out of sunburn. When we arrived, I sprayed the MediQuick on the boys' backs; Chick sprayed my back. She didn't need any spray herself, because her redness turned to tan.

At supper time, I borrowed my dad's car and took Chick out to dinner. We had a great time. The boys, on the other hand, fixed themselves some peanut butter & jelly sandwiches. No one was willing to cook except Mike and me. Mike didn't want the job full time, so he decided it was best not to offer to cook for anyone for any reason.

We left for Porky's at 8:45 pm. I drove Chick there in my dad's car. Once again we were alternating sets with The Thunderbirds. We would try to develop a good rock sound, only to have to stop, and let Billy & Lillie and the Thunderbirds change the mood and atmosphere with their cool blues and jazz tunes. It was really hard trying to create a good rock atmosphere and sound, when we had to start all over each set, like it was our first set of the night. We could not keep the "rock momentum" going because of The Thunderbirds playing a different kind of music every half hour.

As we took to the stage on our fourth set, we could sense something was wrong when Phil sat down on his amp. In all the years The Kingtones played together, Phil had never sat down while playing; he always stood up at the microphone. He next sat on the floor. We wondered if he was having a slight sunstroke from too much sun that day; he looked like he was going to pass out. We stopped playing and helped him off the stage. We laid him on a table and put a cold wet cloth on his head; he passed out. We poured a little water on his face and he came to. We gave him some water to drink and just let him rest. Meanwhile, the Thunderbirds took over and finished our set. They then played their regular alternating set. By the time they were finished, Phil was sitting up and felt well enough to continue playing.

On our last break, I was so tired; I went out to the car and lay down on the seat. The next thing I knew, Pete was shaking me. He said the band was on stage playing their second song without me, and to get my ass in there now! What a night!

When we finished playing, I took Chick back to her apartment. I was very tired and very sad to have to say good bye. As my heart was breaking, I told her that I loved her; I then mustered up a happy appearance and with a smile said I would see her soon. I gave her a long kiss and said good bye. As I walked back to my apartment, tears rolled down my face. I really loved that girl and I was going to miss her terribly.

When I got back, my thoughts of Chick quickly vanished because the boys were talking about different tortures and killings they had heard about or read in the paper. They were also complaining about their sunburn; I got out the MediQuick and sprayed their backs.

Phil said that on Monday, March 16, Porky was going to try out another rock 'n roll band to alternate with us. We decided that if we still couldn't find the "Kingtones' Sound" on Monday night, with only rock music being played, we were going to give Porky our two week notice and leave. We were all starting to feel a little homesick anyway.

Outside of being sunburned, four of us were healthy. We weren't sure about Phil's health because of his passing out at Porky's. We were getting along well.

March 12, 1964 (Thursday)

We got up at 2:30 pm. It was another very hot day, until a ten minute downpour cooled things down a little. Everybody except Pete was moaning and groaning about their sunburn. We took turns spraying each other's back with MediQuick. I don't think it worked very well. The boys helped me clean up the apartment a little bit after I bitched at them, and we took the Kingtones' van back to the Ford Dealership to get the starter fixed.

On the way back to our apartment, I made the boys stop at the store for some groceries. They were not happy about it, but I told them if we didn't stop, I wasn't making supper. When we got back, I made them a nice dinner: round steak, corn, tossed salad, mashed potatoes and Kool-Aid.

At 8:15 pm, we left for Porky's. The Thunderbirds went on stage first that night. We noticed when they started playing, that they didn't sound very good. We then realized that their usual bass player, who we considered the backbone of the band, was missing; he was sick. They had a fill in bass player: probably one of those musicians sitting in the Union Hall waiting to be called, but he wasn't nearly as good. This actually helped us; because The Thunderbirds didn't sound very good, it made our music sound even better. Our "rock momentum" was picking up steam and by the last two sets, the "Kingtones' Sound" was back. The audience stayed to the end and yelled for encores.

When we finished playing, we found out that Porky hadn't even been there to see how well we had done. On our way back to the apartment, Pete started yelling about not getting paid enough. We all felt the same way, but we didn't know exactly what to do about it. We were all healthy and getting along just okay. I missed Chick very much.

March 13, 1964 (Friday)

We got up at noon. It was another hot day. I made breakfast: eggs, sausage, toast, fried potatoes and Kool-Aid. The boys thought they had "died and gone to heaven." This was their first cooked breakfast since Chick had come to Florida.

We got up earlier than what we usually did, because we had to go to Porky's and get our equipment off the stage. Porky was bringing in a special musical group called The Treniers; we did not have to play Friday or Saturday night. When we finished clearing the stage, Porky gave us each a bright yellow Porky's t-shirt with his logo on it. He wanted us to wear them as often as we could to advertise his club. He wanted to make sure that the college kids knew that Porky's was the place to go!

We returned to our apartment and I fixed supper. We were still hurting from our sunburn, so we sprayed some more MediQuick on each other's back. Phil was starting to itch all over. During dinner, we talked about how on Monday, The Kingtones' name was going to take top billing on Porky's huge marquee. We were going to ask Porky if we could put the giant letters up ourselves. The Thunderbirds had the top billing at that time, but they were done playing at Porky's on Sunday night. We also hoped that the band Porky was trying out on Monday was good, so Porky would hire them. Otherwise, we were going to have to play six hours a night; six days a week by ourselves.

We watched TV for a while, and then decided to go to a drive-in movie. Pete wouldn't go because we didn't choose the movie he wanted to see. After the show, we decided to go to Porky's to see The Treniers. On our way there, we ran out of gas. Fortunately, we had passed a gas station a half mile back. After we went and got some gas, we continued on to Porky's. We didn't really care for The Treniers. They were another band like The Thunderbirds, but not nearly as good. They had a lot of good synchronized dance moves, but it wasn't good enough to make up for their mediocre vocals.

I don't know how he got served, but Mike came over to our table acting like a "big man on campus;" he was drinking a Whiskey Sour. I got pissed at him for drinking and chewed him out. It didn't do any good, he just gulped it down. As we were leaving, we saw Paul Hornung sitting up at the bar. He was one of the best halfbacks that ever played football for the Green Bay Packers. I wanted to get his autograph, but I was afraid to ask him for it. We got home exhausted. We were all healthy and getting along fair.

March 14, 1964 (Saturday)

We got up around 12:30 pm; I made breakfast. I was really getting sick of cooking. The boys never offered to help with any of the meals, except for Mike; he would make the Kool-Aid.

Because The Treniers were playing at Porky's and we had the night off, we didn't really know what to do. The boys started off with their usual "TV Watch," while I wrote out a few post cards to send back home. Phil suggested going to Story-Land to look around and wanted to know if anybody wanted to go with him. I jumped at the chance to get out of the apartment; nobody else wanted to go.

When we got there, they were closed. We didn't want to go back to the apartment, so we rode around until 7 o'clock. When we finally returned, we found a note from the boys. It said that they had received a letter from our old neighbor Lloyd. He had invited all of us to Miami, to go swimming in the motel pool of which he now managed. The boys didn't hesitate; they immediately called Lloyd to make sure that it would be okay to go there that day. Lloyd said, "Yes," and Bob, Mike and even Pete went to Miami to visit him.

I fixed supper for Phil and me; then we decided to go to a show. We went and saw Walt Disney's *Fantasia*. I did not like it at all. There was not enough storyline for me, and it had classical music throughout the whole thing, which I was not fond of. Phil, on the other hand, thought it was a masterpiece. He loved the classical music and loved the way it was interwoven amongst the characters' movements.

On our way home, we stopped by Porky's. Porky came over to us and said that we had to come in early the next day to practice with a group of male soul singers.* They were going to sing at his place Sunday night and they needed a band to back them up.

The boys got back to the apartment the same time that Phil and I did. They told us how they went swimming in a big beautiful pool, visited with Lloyd for a while and did a little shopping; they had a great time. On their way back to the apartment, they saw a billboard advertising Porky's, and The Kingtones were on it. They were pretty excited about it. Their excitement was quickly squelched, however, when Phil told Mike and Bob that we had to go in early Sunday to practice with The Soulmen, so they could sing Sunday night. They needed a backup band, and we were it. We got along well that day, because all five of us were not together. Everyone was healthy.

Because no one in The Kingtones could remember the name of the male soul singers, for future reference to this group, we will call them "The Soulmen."

March 15, 1964 (Sunday)

I got up at 11:30 am. Once again it was a very hot day. Since it was too late for church, I went back to bed. At one o'clock I woke up again; I got up and made dinner: steak, mashed potatoes, yellow beans, fried onions, Kool-Aid and fruit cocktail for dessert. We ate at 3:00 pm. When we finished eating, the boys immediately left the table to watch TV. Although I finally got the lazy bums to do the dishes, I had to clear the table. They refused to help with that.

We went to Porky's to set our equipment back up. It was two hours of torture. We then practiced with The Soulmen. It was almost a nightmare. They were excellent singers, but we didn't know any of their songs. I was writing musical chords and notes all over the place. We finally learned enough tunes for a forty minute set and called it a day. We had the feeling that this was going to be a disaster.

That night, we took to the stage first. We played our usual half hour and then The Thunderbirds played their half hour. Starting the third set, we brought up The Soulmen. They seemed to "come alive" with an audience in front of them. They sounded great, and had some good choreography that went with their singing; they were a big hit! We were not only shocked by how good they were, but surprised at how good we sounded backing them up.

This was Billy and Lillie & the Thunderbirds last night. We had mixed emotions about their leaving. We did think that if only rock music was played at Porky's, we could get the "Kingtones' Sound" most of the time. We felt that this would result in packing the place with college kids, and keeping them there most of the night. On the other hand, Billy and Lillie were a class act. The Thunderbirds were very professional, great musicians and nice guys. We had learned a lot about showmanship and stage presence from them. We were going to miss them. At the end of the night, we said good bye and thanked them for everything they had taught us.

We finally got up enough courage and went and told Porky we wanted a raise. We felt that since we were doing extra practice and backing up other groups, we deserved more money. Porky said he would pay us $550.00 for the week, but we had to play an extra night for it. Since we had more time than money, we accepted his offer. We were now going to play seven nights a week.

We left and went to the Royal Castle for something to eat. By the time we got home it was 5:30 am. Needless to say we were very tired. We were all healthy and got along only fairly well that day.

March 16, 1964 (Monday)

We got up at 12:50 pm. The weather outside was very comfortable: not too hot. We got dressed, ate a quick breakfast and left for Porky's. We had to practice with The Soulmen once again; we practiced all afternoon.

When we finished practicing, Porky asked us if we wanted to put our name out on his Marquee; he didn't have to ask us twice. We took a twelve foot ladder and some jumbo letters, and went out to the giant neon sign! There we put "Tonight – THE KINGTONES". We were so excited and proud; we took all kinds of pictures of it. That was quite a thrill for us: seeing our name in lights!

When we were done with the marquee, we went back to our apartment. I called Chick and talked to her for a while. It was so nice to hear her voice; I really missed her. I fixed a quick supper and we watched TV until it was time to go play.

We left for Porky's at 8:45 pm. Porky was trying out another rock band that night. We couldn't wait to hear them and hoped they were good. We wanted Porky to hire them so we wouldn't have to play all six hours by ourselves. Porky had the other band go on first. They weren't necessarily the worst band that we ever heard, but they were darn close to it. We couldn't imagine Porky hiring them. Not only did he not hire them, but as soon as they had finished their half hour set, Porky told them to get their equipment off the stage and to "Get Out!" We had to finish playing the entire night: all five of the forty minute sets. Boy, were we mad!

When we finished playing, we went and told Porky to either pay us more money or give us fewer hours. We said that six hours for one band to play was just too much. It looked like Porky was giving our ultimatum serious consideration until Mike, a.k.a. "Clod," spoke up. He said, "Well, we played fire hours at The Club Ponytail; we can do six here." So that killed any chance of Porky compromising with us. By the time we got out of Porky's and back to our apartment, it was 5:30 am. We were very tired, healthy and getting along pretty well.

March 17, 1964 (Tuesday)

We got up at two o'clock. The weather was a little cooler with a nice breeze. It felt good after so many days of very hot temperatures. Because it was so nice out, everybody, except Bob, wanted to get out of the apartment: I went and bought groceries; Mike and Phil went to a hobby shop and bought a chess game and two model airplanes to put together; Pete went and bought some new shoes; Bob stayed home and watched TV.

When everyone returned, I made a big supper. After we finished eating, Phil and Mike started putting their model airplanes together. The rest of us watched TV until we had to leave for Porky's. We use to have Tuesdays off, but under our new agreement with Porky, we now played seven nights a week.

Our theory about playing only rock and roll music at Porky's, to help us get the "Kingtones' Sound," was put to the test that night, and it seemed to be true. Our first two forty minute sets were good; the middle two forty minute sets were excellent; the last two sets were great. Pete was at the top of his game. His vocals were superb; he called the right songs at the right time. He moved around and danced a little. I bounced on my chair so much, I thought I might break it. I even told a few stupid jokes that I learned from my mentor Doc Jorne'. The audience seemed to love those stupid jokes; they laughed and clapped. Bob and Phil had their sound down and were swinging their guitars in sync with the music. Mike was fabulous on the drums that night. His driving beat made you dance, even if you didn't really want to. The music all came together and the crowd loved us. They stayed until we finished.

When we were done, we headed to Royal Castle to get something to eat. Pete started to say that he thought he should make more money than the rest of us. He indicated that our successful night was because of him. I took issue with him and told him what each of us had done to make the night successful. He was getting a "big head" and hard to get along with. He said he was thinking of leaving and going back to Michigan. That ended our discussion. We got back to our apartment at 5:30 am. We were exhausted; six hours a night was just too much. I said a prayer and thanked God for our success that night.

Four of us were healthy; Mike was coming down with a cold. We were not getting along very well, especially not with Pete.

March 18, 1964 (Wednesday)

We got up at two o'clock; we were still very tired. It was another very nice day outside: 78 degrees. I made breakfast and then all of us, except Pete, went to the hobby shop. We looked around for a little while, but nobody bought anything. We returned to our apartment and watched TV until supper time. I called Chick and then fixed dinner: Chili Con Carne.

We left for Porky's at 8:45 pm. We started playing to a small crowd. The combination of being tired, along with very few people in attendance, affected our sound and stage presence; the first two hours we were just mediocre. But as the crowd continued to build, our enthusiasm came back and the "Kingtones' Sound" surfaced. Once again we "tore" the place up! The last four hours, we were terrific! I never bounced so much in my life and the audience seemed to eat it up.

During one of our breaks, an A & R man for Capital Records approached us and wanted to sign us to a record contract. We told him we were already signed to Liberty Records, but thanked him for the offer. He said he was going to talk to his dad about buying our contract from Liberty, because we were the greatest band he had seen in years. Even though we thought this guy was feeding us a line of bull, just trying to make himself look important, we wanted to leave him with positive thoughts about us, just in case what he said was true; we said that we looked forward to hearing from him.

When we finished playing, we went to Royal Castle. We didn't talk very much on the way there because we were so tired; six hours a night was taking its toll on us. It was hard to be energetic seven days a week; six hours a night. Pete's voice was starting to get a little hoarse. We were going to be in real trouble if he couldn't sing for a night or two. We were all healthy and getting along alright.

March 19, 1964 (Thursday)

We got up at three o'clock. The day was once again beautiful: sunny, 75 degrees with a nice little breeze. When our mail arrived that day, we had quite a scare. After our recording session on February 6, we took the master tape to our next record, *The Girl I Love*, with us to Florida. Phil had mailed the master tape, along with a letter inside the package, to our record company two weeks ago. What we got in the mail, was the letter that Phil had sent with the recording, but no sign of the master tape. Phil immediately called Cadet Distributing, to see if by some miracle, they happened to have received the tape. Detroit said that they had received the tape, but there was no letter with it. They had already released the record on the West Coast, and it was doing very well out there; that was a big relief off our minds. We were thrilled that our record had been released already and that it was doing well.

Mike and Phil continued to put their model airplanes together. Bob decided that he liked the idea of putting a model together and so he went to the hobby shop and bought himself a plastic model gun. The apartment looked like a pigsty, but the boys didn't seem to care. They had model building to do; there was no time for cleaning. I couldn't stand it, so I took off to the beach and bought some trinkets. When I got back, I made supper. We then watched TV until we had to go play.

When we got to Porky's, the place was dead. We figured this was the "Calm before the Storm." Friday was the beginning of College Spring Break and we expected many more students to be there. But this was Thursday, the last dead night we hoped. Pete decided he was going to get the few customers that were there to clap and cheer. He started with some of his "kick ass" vocals: no one clapped. He started kicking his legs in the air and dancing across the stage: no one clapped. He jumped, hopped, bounced, anything he could think of, but not one lousy clap resulted from his effort. When we finally took a break, Pete went and got himself half drunk. It seemed like the longest night we ever played.

When we finished playing, we went to Royal Castle. There we told Homer, the chief cook, waiter and bottle washer of the restaurant, how Pete had tried to get the audience to clap. Homer just laughed and gave Pete a standing ovation. We got home at 5:30 am. We were dead tired, all healthy and getting along okay.

March 20, 1964 (Friday)

We got up at 3:15 pm. It was a rather warm day, in spite of the fact that the sky was overcast and it had been raining all morning. Phil's grandma came over to our apartment to see him. She took him and Mike out for a day of fun. We were all jealous. I fixed breakfast for Pete, Bob and me. When we finished, Pete and I went to Porky's to get some posters advertising Porky's Night Club for our van. Bob didn't want to go. He was going to get his hair cut and wanted to start putting his model gun together.

When Pete and I got to Porky's, we noticed a canoe by the small manmade lake next to the side of the club. Porky also had a small Pirate Ship by the water, with a gangplank sticking out the back. After getting the signs, we asked Porky if we could take his canoe for a ride and climb on the pirate ship. Porky gave us some canoe paddles and said to go at it. We canoed for about a half hour and then climbed the pirate ship; we even walked the gangplank. We had a great time.

When we got back to the apartment, I made dinner for Pete, Bob and me: barbecue. Before we had a chance to sit down and eat, Phil and Mike came back. They had a very boring day. All they did was drive around all afternoon with grandma. Mike was so bored, he didn't want to go to supper with them, so I volunteered and took his place. While Pete, Bob and Mike chowed down on their barbecues, Phil and I went to a beautiful restaurant called "The Roundtable." There we ordered steak and mushrooms. The atmosphere was magnificent and the food terrific. Mike really lost out on a great meal.

We left for Porky's at 8:45 pm. We did not know if we would have a big audience or not. Although this was considered the first "official" night of college spring break, many students would be in transit and wouldn't be there yet. We began playing to a rather small crowd. We were a little loud and not in balance; because of this, the first three sets were not very good. Phil finally figured out what was wrong. He told us to turn down and to keep in balance. That did the trick. The "Kingtones' Sound" surfaced and we rocked the place.

Starting with the fourth set, Pete put on a display of showmanship that even impressed us. His vocals were superb and he danced, moved and bounced all over the place. This made the night go fairly fast. We weren't nearly as tired as we had been on Thursday, when we finished that night. Although the crowd never got very big, the students that were there said they would be back with their friends.

As we left for our apartment, Bob and Mike told us to go on without them, they said they had a couple of "Hot Dates!" So Pete, Phil and I left. We did not stop at Royal Castle; we just went straight home. When we got there, we had some snacks and got ready for bed. Before we even got to our bed, Mike and Bob were back with their hot dates who were dropping them off. Although the boys didn't get what they were hoping for, they did get a free breakfast so they weren't totally disappointed. When we asked Mike if he had any luck "scoring" with his girl, he said no, but he wasn't really sure why.

He said he asked her, "Do you like to play keep away?"
She answered, "Why?"
He said, "Because you're keeping away from me!"

That was the end of Mike's romantic evening. We were all healthy and getting along well.

March 21, 1964 (Saturday)

We got up at four o'clock. Because it was so late in the day, I made myself a snack and then started supper. The boys watched TV, ate supper, put on their band uniforms and left for Porky's. What a waste of a day.

Porky was trying out another new band that day. They were called "The Situations." He wanted to have two rock bands playing all the time during spring break. The crowd was bigger than Friday night, but many of the students that were coming were still not there. "The Situations" played the first set. They were a lot better than the last band Porky tried out; at least he didn't ask them to pack up and leave.

When it was our turn to take the stage, we seemed once again, to have sound problems. We tried Friday night's "cure" of turning down and getting in balance, but it didn't help much. This was the first time that we had shared the stage with another band for any length of time since "The Thunderbirds." We started to think that maybe we just couldn't adjust to following another band. Needless to say, we were only mediocre. The good news for us was that "The Situations" weren't any better.

Then out of the blue came Dave Roberts, Phil's brother. He was there, for spring break, with all his rowdy friends that loved The Kingtones. They hollered, yelled and cheered after every song we played, like we were the greatest. Regardless of how we sounded, I still bounced like a crazy man and Mike continued his powerful driving drum beat. Because of all the excitement from Dave's groupies, along with Mike and I acting like everything was great, the audience thought we were pretty good.

When we finished playing for the night, Bob told us not to wait for him and Pete; they had a couple of "Hot Dates!" We told Bob we had heard that story before, and evidently his definition of hot and our definition of hot were two different things. Mike, Phil and I left. We did not stop at Royal Castle but went straight to our apartment. Bob and Pete didn't get home until 8:00 am. Once again their dates had different ideas of what a good time was, and the boys struck out again. We were all healthy and getting along satisfactory.

March 22, 1964 (Sunday)

We got up at 1:30 pm. It was a nice day out: 75 degrees. I had missed church once again, but even when I did make it, I was usually so tired that I didn't understand a word the preacher said anyway.

Bob and Pete had talked their dates from last night, to go on another date with them to a baseball game. So the boys picked them up and went to see the Tigers play the Yankees. The Tigers won the game: 6 to 0. Mike took off to see Lloyd in Miami. Phil and I went canoeing and fishing at Porky's man-made lake. We stopped at a store on our way and bought two 89 cent fishing poles from the Kiddy Department. I told Phil that we would never catch any fish with those stupid fishing poles. He assured me that the fish wouldn't know the difference. We caught fifteen little fish; I couldn't believe it.

We got back to the apartment around 7:30 pm; everybody was there. Mike said he had a great time with Lloyd. Bob and Pete were in the mood for Mexican food, so they went out for dinner. I made spaghetti and fried lunch meat for the rest of us.

We left for Porky's at 8:45 pm. When we got there, the line to get in the club went out the door: THE COLLEGE STUDENTS HAD ARRIVED! We started the first set at 9:30 pm. Since we had six half hours to play, we started off playing some of our more moderate rockers. The students didn't seem to care; they screamed and hollered like every song was great.

The Situations came on at 10 pm. Things cooled down a little bit with their music. They were not as good as we were. We came back on at 10:30 pm and once again the crowd started to go nuts. With the "Kingtones' Sound" in place, we got better and better each set. Mike's driving beat, assisted by Bob's pounding bass and Phil's gritty guitar sound turned the students into "animals." I bounced, once again, like a crazy man! My head was constantly shaking with my Beatle like hair flying all over the place. We were terrific!

During our breaks and at the end of the night, all kinds of kids came up to us to get our phone number and address for out of state jobs. We figured that we would probably never get a call from any of them, but it made us feel good anyway. We were all healthy and getting along well.

March 23, 1964 (Monday)

Mike, Phil and I got up at three o'clock; Pete and Bob stayed in bed. It was another very pleasant day outside. Mike and Phil decided to go to Miami to see if they could find some parts for Phil's Thunderbird. I stayed at the apartment and cleaned.

When Phil and Mike got back, we decided to go fishing at Porky's Lake. Mike said he would paddle the canoe so that Phil and I could troll and catch fish. As our fishing expedition began, with our 89 cent fishing poles, Mike started to paddle. What seemed like a good idea at first, having Mike paddle so we could troll for fish, turned out not to be so good. Mike was paddling so fast that our worms were skimming along on top of the water. Phil and I didn't get a single bite, much less any fish. We told Mike he either had to paddle much slower or he couldn't paddle at all. Mike paddled the canoe to shore and got out. The bad news was that Mike was pissed; the good news was that Phil and I started catching all kinds of fish by just sitting in one spot.

Bob and Pete finally got out of bed and decided that they wanted to eat supper out. They stopped by Porky's to see if the three of us wanted to join them; so the five of us went out for dinner. After we ordered, we talked about Sunday night's performance: what was good, bad, changes that should be made, new things we should try, etc. Before we knew it, an hour had passed and we didn't have our food yet. We waved down our waitress and told her that if we didn't get our food in the next ten minutes, we were leaving. By the time we finished eating and got back to our apartment it was 8:50 pm. We changed into our uniform and flew to Porky's.

When we got to Porky's, the line to get in was once again out the door. When we got inside, the place was packed. As we took to the stage, the crowd roared! Screamed! Clapped! And hollered: Michigan State students, whom The Kingtones had been playing for over the past six months were there in force: we could do no wrong!

Every song we played, the crowd went crazy. The "Kingtones' Sound" was loud and clear. Pete was at his best; with Phil's driving guitar, Mike's powerful beat, Bob's booming bass and old crazy me bouncing and jumping around on the keyboards, we had the place going wild. The students danced like mad fools. Some of them had to be taken off of the table tops by the bouncers, because they were dancing on them. It was mass hysteria!

When The Situations came on stage, they were a little intimidated. It was probably a good thing that they came on when they did, or the place might have been torn apart. The Situations took the edge off the crowd a little bit and calmed things down.

As soon as we came back on again, "Michigan State" started chanting, "The Bird," "The Bird." We did a crazy rendition of *Surfin' Bird*, a.k.a. *"The Bird,"* by the Trashmen. It was a huge audience favorite at the Coral Gables in Lansing, Michigan, where The Kingtones had been playing, and they wanted to hear it. When we played it, the place went crazy! You couldn't hear yourself think! When we finished the song, they yelled, "More! More!" insistently; they wouldn't stop. So we played it a second time. The place went ballistic!! It's hard to express in words how good we were that night or how the audience reacted to us. We sounded like a national recording group and looked and acted like professionals.

We held the crowd so well that some of the students waiting outside to get in never did. When we finished at 3:30 am, the audience yelled "More!" "Encore!" "Do *The Bird* again!" "Encore!" Before we left the stage, Porky had us make an announcement that on Tuesday night, if you had an M.S.U. picture I.D. card, you could get into Porky's without paying a cover charge. This brought about more mass hysteria!!

As we left the stage, the owner of Lenny's, Porky's number one rival, came over and offered us a job playing at his place. Porky's had now become the number one club to go to because of The Kingtones; Lenny wanted us. He said he would pay us more money than what Porky was paying us. I don't know if he remembered at the time, but we had tried to audition for his place before we went to Porky's. Lenny himself said he already had a band for spring break and wouldn't even listen to us. Because of this, Phil told him no; we were staying at Porky's. This was the first year that Porky's became the number one club in Fort Lauderdale.

As we were leaving, Porky came over, smiled and said, "You guys were good tonight." That's about the best compliment you could get out of Porky. We wanted him to say ".... you guys were awesome, magnificent, terrific, fabulous, etc." But from Porky, "good" was as good as it was going to get. He continued by saying that he was going to start running an afternoon jam session, starting Thursday, from 5:00 pm to 7:00 pm. He wanted us to start advertising it on stage tomorrow night. We couldn't believe it. Not only were we already playing seven nights a week, starting Thursday, we were going to start playing twice a day. Porky wasn't done yet; he said he wanted us to come in later that day to practice with another singing group that he was going to let perform at his club, but they needed a backup band. They were called the African Beatles. This was starting to feel a little like a "Chinese Sweatshop." I thought to myself that I wouldn't be able to survive at the pace we were going.

When we got back to the apartment, I wanted to write Chick a letter. I had been so busy lately, that my letter writing to her was falling behind. I wanted to her tell how well we were doing at Porky's and how much I missed her. I was so tired however, I fell asleep with the pencil in my hand. We were all healthy and getting along well.

March 24, 1964 (Tuesday)

We got up at 2:45 pm. It was another beautiful day outside. Phil and I went to the Musicians' Union in Miami to pay our work dues. Phil dropped me off by the front door and told me he would be waiting for me in the back. After walking through the "Gymnasium of Unemployed Musicians," I paid The Kingtones' work dues and quickly slipped out the back door. The parking lot was very full, but I didn't see Phil. So I waited and waited, but he didn't come. I couldn't imagine what happened to him. After an hour's wait, I walked around to the front of the building and there he was. I said, "You told me you would be in the back of the building, what happened?" Phil said it was too hot in the back, so he moved to the front.

When we got back to our apartment, I noticed that Bob still hadn't done his own dishes from Monday. I yelled at him for being so lazy. Since we had to be at Porky's early to practice with the African Beatles, he was not going to have time to do them until Wednesday. We grabbed a quick sandwich, grabbed our uniforms and headed to Porky's.

Practicing with the African Beatles was much easier than practicing with The Soulmen because we already knew a bunch of Beatles' songs. We practiced until about eight pm. We quit then because the college kids were pouring in and wanted us to start playing. They had come early to make sure they could get in.

We had brought our uniforms, so we didn't have to go back to the apartment. We went to the band room, changed into our uniforms and stayed there until it was time to go play. We didn't want the students to see us for fear that they would start chanting, "We want the band," and Porky would make us go on early.

At 9:30 pm, we had The Situations go on first. We figured that because their music was a little tamer than ours, this would help keep "the lid" on the wild students a little longer. We came on stage at ten o'clock. The crowd was not as crazy as they had been Monday night, thanks to our new strategy of starting with The Situations.

We started with some of our lighter rock tunes. This was to continue managing the crowd. At 10:30 pm, The Situations continued their "crowd controlling" music. At 11:00 pm, we brought up The African Beatles. They were not as good as The Soulmen, but they were unique and sounded decent. This was a change of pace, also directed at crowd control.

We knew sooner or later we would have to do *"The Bird."* We figured this would probably make the students go nuts, so we saved it until the last set. When we finally did the song, it was great! I bounced and jumped so much, I ripped my pants all apart. The crowd went wild. They screamed! And yelled! And clapped! When we finished the song, they started yelling, "More!" "More *Bird!*" but we quickly started playing a slow song and that finally squelched the diehard *Bird* lovers. We were not as electrifying that night as we had been on Monday night, but that was by design.

When we finished for the night, we headed to Royal Castle, all of us except Pete. He had a date and was flying solo. We were all healthy and getting along pretty well, except Bob and me. I was pissed at him for not doing his dishes.

March 25, 1964 (Wednesday)

We got up at four o'clock. Pete and Mike went to Ft. Lauderdale to a beach shindig. I don't know if Mike was trying to impress some girls or Pete, but he started drinking beer. He drank until he got drunk. When he finally threw up, Pete dragged him out of the party and went back to the apartment.

Bob, Phil and I went to listen to a new band that was starting at Porky's that night. They were called The Percussions. They were from Chicago and they had played for Porky before. It was hard to tell if the band was any good because they were missing one of their band members: the keyboard player. He had a prior commitment and wouldn't be able to join the group until Friday. The lead singer, however, was terrific; he was as good as Pete. He sang Dee Clark's hit song, *Raindrops*, as good if not better than Dee Clark. It was going to be an interesting night. We introduced ourselves to them, and Frank, the lead singer, asked me if I would sit in with them for the next two nights. I didn't want to, because I was already playing six half hours a night. If I said yes, I would be playing six hours a night with no breaks. But Frank was a great guy, with a "silver tongue," and he talked me into it.

We returned to our apartment where we found Mike half drunk and half sick. I got mad at both Mike and Pete: Mike for drinking and Pete for letting it happen. I told Major if he didn't do his dishes, I wouldn't fix supper. Since Bob was hungry, he did his dishes; I fixed supper.

We left for Porky's at 8:45 pm. Mike wasn't in the best shape to drum, but he was all we had. The Percussions and I went on the first half hour. Frank knew how to work an audience. With his smooth talking manner, you couldn't help but like him. His voice was so good that even though the band didn't sound that good, it wasn't that noticeable. The Kingtones went on at ten o'clock, with a woozy drummer. Needless to say Mike's usual hard driving beat was not there. In fact, we were lucky he could play at all. The first two hours for both bands were not that impressive.

Mike, trying to get his head on straight, got some tomato juice to drink while he was drumming. Since he had no where to put the glass while he drummed, he placed it on the edge of my organ top. It was only a matter of minutes before my bouncing vibrated the glass to fall off. The tomato juice landed on my organ tubes and blew them out; my organ was out of commission. Porky did have a piano close by, but it was not on the stage and it was not electric. Phil put a microphone by the piano and I played it, but it couldn't be heard very well; it was more or less useless.

Fortunately for us, the Michigan State students knew we were having problems and hooted and hollered like we were good anyway. On our last set, the crowd started chanting, "The Bird, The Bird." Because most of the audience had been patient with all of our mishaps, I came up on stage and we did *"The Bird."* I was able to go nuts on stage because I wasn't behind my organ. I jumped, bounced, was down on my knees, down on my belly and back up again. The students ate it up! When we finished the song, they yelled "More! More!" so I did something special for them that I hadn't done in years. I did a mock impersonation of Elvis, singing *Long Tall Sally*. I had the curled lip, the black hair, along with wild and crazy gyrations. I shook, wiggled, danced, jumped, and did a flip; everything I could think of. When we finished the song, the place went ballistic. They were screaming at the top of their lungs for "More!" but I was so tired, I could hardly stand, much less do another encore. When our nightmare evening finally ended, our only salvation was we left the stage on a "high note." The students were patting us on the back saying how great we were.

Phil, Mike and I went to Royal Castle. Bob and Pete had some hot dates and did not go with us. When we finally got back to our apartment, the doors were locked. Pete and Bob had brought their dates to our apartment. We beat on the door. Pete came to the door in the dark naked. He told us to go away and to come back in fifteen minutes. So we sat out in The Kingtones van and watched the clock. Fifteen minutes later, we pounded on the door again. Bob unlocked the door as the four of them hurried to get dressed. We were all a little pissed at Pete and Bob for using our apartment for their extra circular activities. We were all absolutely exhausted and couldn't wait to go to bed and to be locked out was more then we could take. Pete claimed that he hit a "Home Run" with his date, while Bob only got to second base. What a night!

March 26, 1964 (Thursday)

Phil and I got up at 10:30 am, after getting to bed at 5:30 am. We went to Porky's and called an organ repairman. He came over, cleaned the sockets that held the organ tubes, and replaced all the blown tubes from Mike's tomato juice. I also bought several spare tubes in case they would go out some other time. His repair bill was $16.98. We took that out of Mike's pay for that week. That was an expensive glass of tomato juice!

We returned to the apartment, ate a quick lunch, got dressed in white Levi's and yellow Porky t-shirts, and left for our first afternoon Jam Session: 5:00 pm to 7:00 pm. Porky was expecting a good crowd, because he had advertised $1.50 for all the beer men could drink, and $1.00 for all the beer the ladies could drink.

Needless to say, the place was packed when we got there. We started off playing a lot of "kicker" type songs so that the kids would really enjoy the jam session. They enjoyed it all right; they were like "savages." There were four different times when it looked like a fight was breaking out, but the bouncers were "Johnny on the spot," and prevented them from taking place. They finally did throw two guys out and told them to never come back. We played two forty minute sets. The kids loved the music. They danced like wild animals; they were almost uncontrollable.

When seven o'clock came, we got off the stage and ran to our cars. We did not want to do any encores or socialize. We had to be back to play at

9:30 pm, and we needed quiet time and rest. We went back to our apartment. While the boys plopped down to watch TV, I called Chick. It was nice talking to her; she always gave me peace of mind. When I finished, I went and bought some groceries. I came back, made a quick supper; we got dressed in our Kingtones' suits and left for Porky's.

When we arrived at Porky's, the line to get in was huge. Evidently, a lot of the students that came to the jam session never left. Our first set went very well. The students, as usual, screamed and yelled after most of our songs. I filled in, once again, on the keyboards for The Percussions. Their keyboard player wasn't coming to play until Friday. They also did well on their first set. I played organ for 3 ½ hours straight, with no break. Just as it looked like we were really going to rock the place, Pete went hoarse. He couldn't sing any more. The good news was that Frank, from The Percussions, offered to help out; He was a great singer. The bad news was that Frank did not know most of our songs. We tried to do some songs that he knew, but we didn't really know those songs.

Besides Pete being out of commission, Mike was having one of the worst nights that he ever had on the drums. He would stop in the wrong places; his tempo would speed up then slow down on the same song and he would end the songs too soon. I don't know if his hangover was giving him trouble, but it was not a good night for him or us.

We brought up the African Beatles, three different times to help save the day; they had a hard time getting their harmonies right. Their first two sets were only satisfactory; they finally got it together to have a good last set.

When we finished for the night, Pete, Phil and I went back to our apartment. Bob and Mike, once again, had some hot dates. Bob was tired of only getting to second base, so he picked a girl that acted like she really wanted a good time. As Bob pursued his "home run fantasy," he found out that his girl had her "monthly friend" with her! She wouldn't allow him a "Grand Slam!" She did the next best thing however; she grabbed Bob's "joy stick," and started exercising it. Bob thought he was in heaven until her sharp finger nails cut into his joy stick making this a kind of masochistic experience. Mike, as usual, struck out. We were all healthy, except we weren't sure about Bob's joy stick, and we were getting along fairly well.

March 27, 1964 (Friday)

We got up at 4:50 pm; we had overslept. We found a note from Mike and Pete saying that they got up early and went to another beach shindig. They said they would see us at the jam session. It was a rather gloomy and cool day outside. We hoped that the beach party would be cut short because of it. Since we had to be at Porky's at 5:00 pm, we threw on our clothes and left immediately.

We got to Porky's twenty minutes late. Porky was mad at us, but he didn't say much. Mike was there waiting for us. I was about to yell at him again, when he told us that he didn't drink any alcohol at the party. When we asked where Pete was, he said that he needed to rest his vocal cords and wasn't coming; he would see us at the 9:30 pm performance. Since Pete sang about 75% of our songs, and did 100% of all the new current tunes, we knew we were in for a long hard jam session.

Before we started, we made an announcement that Pete had gone hoarse last night, and he wouldn't be singing at the jam session that day. A group of guys out in the audience offered up one of their buddies to sit in and sing. We didn't want him to, but they were insistent. So "Joe Crudface" came up and did some singing. He was not good! But his buddies loved the fact that he was up on the stage, and cheered and hooted for him after each crappy song. So we kept him up there for half of each set. That took the pressure off of us, or so we thought. But because the guys were making such a fuss over their buddy, and even singing along with him from the floor, they were not dancing. What they were doing was drinking lots of beer; Porky was not happy about that.

Our nighttime performance was a whole new ball game. Pete was there and his voice was back. Mike was feeling good and was back with his powerful drum beat. In fact, he kicked his bass drum so hard, he broke his foot pedal. He borrowed The Percussions foot pedal and broke that one too. Fortunately, The Percussions drummer carried a spare; he wasn't too anxious to let Mike use it, but he did. Once again we had a fabulous night. The "Kingtones' Sound" was alive and well. The students went from excited, to wild, to crazy, to savages!

We brought up the African Beatles three different times. Each time they came up, they were a hit. They were upset about Thursday night's performance and spent half the day working on their harmonies. They were much better and the audience really liked them.

Once again *"The Bird"* was the big hit of the evening. We saved it until the last set because we didn't really want to do it twice. We thought if we played it early in the night, the students would start yelling towards the end of the night to do it again.

When we finished playing, the place was still packed. We could hardly get off the stage because the floor was so filled with people. As we headed for the door, the kids were patting us on the back saying that we were the greatest band that they had ever seen.

The five of us left together for the first time in a while. The boys didn't have any hot dates that night. We figured that after Bob's masochistic episode, he probably needed a break. We stopped at Royal Castle for a bite to eat. We were all healthy and getting along well.

March 28, 1964 (Saturday)

We got up at 4:30 pm. Once again it was a mad dash to get dressed and make it to Porky's on time for the jam session. Pete had taken off to another beach party and wasn't coming to the afternoon performance. Porky was working us to death. We were starting to get physically run down. This wasn't exactly the "exciting life" that we had envisioned when coming to Fort Lauderdale. It seemed more like we were in a concentration camp.

We arrived at Porky's just in time to go on stage. The place was packed once again, but it was about 80% guys. There were very few ladies present. As we started to play, we noticed that the guys were into showing off and not really listening to us. They were having contests and challenges. There was the Chug-a-lug contest and Follow the Leader on the dance floor, doing the worm, the duck, the snake; all kinds of crazy stunts. They didn't seem interested in the few girls that were there; they were into themselves. It really didn't matter what the band did, as long as we kept the music going. They weren't in the mood for dancing, they just wanted to act crazy and show off. Because they were doing all sorts of challenges and exploits, they weren't drinking much beer. At the price of $1.50 for all the beer you could drink, and not drinking much, that made Porky very happy.

We finished the jam session at seven o'clock, and went back to our apartment to rest and relax. Pete was there when we arrived. He and Bob went out for hamburgers and I made spaghetti for the rest of us.

At 8:45 pm, we left for Porky's. When we got there, the line to get in was once again huge. All the crazy guys from the afternoon jam session were still there. As we went on stage, we noticed that the afternoon jam session attitude of not caring about the band was still present. As we finished each song, we would get a few claps and a few yells, but nothing like we had the first few nights of spring break. We sounded good, but because we didn't get much audience reaction, it was hard to get enthused and play our best.

When we brought up the African Beatles, the crowd was very receptive to them. They were basically doing a singing show, where you could just sit and enjoy watching them. Most of the students didn't dance when they were on, even though they could have. This was the kind of crowd we were facing; they were not in the mood to dance, but just wanted to sit and be entertained. The African Beatles didn't let them down. They put on a good show and sounded terrific.

Although we were glad the African Beatles did well, it made us take a look at what was happening to us. We were a dance band. Our job was to play for people to dance. But here we were, playing back up music to several different groups that didn't have a band. Those groups were not helping us to get people to dance, they were shows in themselves. We were getting a little frustrated with the whole situation.

When we finished for the night, Mike, Phil and I went to Royal Castle. Bob and Pete had dates. Did you notice that I didn't say "Hot Dates?" These two girls seemed very nice and kind; they laughed a lot. I wasn't sure why Pete and Bob decided to take these two girls out, but perhaps they wanted a change. When we got back to the apartment, we noticed Bob's car was there. We could see the four of them in our apartment, because the lights were on. I was getting ready to scream at them if those doors were locked. The doors were not locked. The girls had made a giant Easter basket filled with all kinds of goodies for the whole band, and they wanted to give it to all of us personally. I got my camera out, took a picture of it and went to bed. We were all healthy and getting along well.

March 29, 1964 (Sunday)

We got up at 4:10 pm; the day was overcast and a little gloomy. We figured this would be a good day for our jam session because the sun wasn't out. We left for Porky's for our afternoon "fun." Pete came along today because we threatened to dock his pay for not playing the jam sessions. It was a rather calm afternoon, and the crowd was a little smaller then what it had been on our other jam sessions. We figured that was because spring break, for many of the students, was over that day; some of them were on their way home already. We played a rather conservative two hours and had Pete sing only half of the time.

At seven o'clock, everybody expect Pete, went back to our apartment. Pete said he was going to some party with a friend he met. When we got home, I made beef stew for supper; we watched a little TV and at 8:45 pm went back to Porky's. When we got to Porky's, there was no line out the door, but the place was basically full. Pete was not there yet, so we went on stage and played our first set without him. We were thankful it was only a half hour set. Pete finally arrived at 10:30 pm. He said his friend was supposed to bring him to Porky's at nine o'clock, but never showed up to get him until 10:00 pm. It was kind of a "blah" night. We were tired and worn out and so were the students. Our sound was okay, but our energy level, to make things happen, was about gone.

Although the African Beatles had been going over very well at Porky's, they had a bad habit of showing up late. This was the case on March 29. Porky was so mad at them for being late again, he would not let them go on, and he docked their pay. We were actually glad they weren't going on because we hated backing them up. It was a lot of extra work for us, and there was no extra pay involved with it.

During one of our breaks, a man came over to us and said he owned a bar on an island in Nantucket, Massachusetts. He wanted us to play there during the summer. We figured it was another line of bull, but just in case, we gave him our phone number and address. We said for him to give us a call in May, if he was still interested in having us play at his bar; we would then talk about what it would take to get us there.

When we finished playing for the night, Pete told us not to wait for him or Phil, because they had dates. Pete had met a girl at the party he went to earlier, and she had a friend who liked Phil. This was very upsetting to me. Phil was the only member of the band that I got along with 100% of the time. I only got along with Bob, 50% of the time. To give up Phil for Bob was almost more then I could take, but there was nothing I could do about it.

So Mike, Bob and I went to Royal Castle and then home to bed. Meanwhile, Phil and Pete took their dates back to the girls' apartment. They both got a good night kiss and then…… "I'll see you tomorrow." I don't know about Phil, but I think Pete was hoping for a little more than just a good night kiss. We were all fairly healthy, except Mike who was fighting a cold, and we were getting along well.

March 30, 1964 (Monday)

We got up at 2:30 pm. It was a very nice day outside and the sun was shining. It was an extra nice day for us, because we didn't have to play the jam session. We talked Porky into having The Percussions play it. Because Porky had agreed to pay us $25.00 for each jam session, even though we hadn't seen any of the money yet, he was having us play all of them. We convinced him, however, that a little break from playing, so we could rest and relax, would help us do a much better job at night; we told him to pay the The Percussions the $25.00.

Phil and Pete took off with the girls that they had dated last night, and went to the beach. Mike, Bob and I decided to go to Miami and visit the seaquarium. This was a thirty-eight acre tropical paradise where we saw dolphins walk on water and killer whales fly through the air. We also saw some excellent marine animal shows. The three of us got along great and we had a wonderful time.

On our way back to our apartment, we found a McDonald's. It was the only McDonald's that we had seen in Florida. There were Burger Kings all over the place, but McDonald's was just coming in. We stopped and I bought seven hamburgers at 15 cents each, and a large coke; we chowed down. We got back to our apartment at seven o'clock. Pete and Phil were already there. We watched TV for a while and then left for Porky's.

When we got to Porky's, there was no line out the door, but on the inside it was packed. We felt refreshed and full of energy. We started out with a bang, and got things jumping right away. The "Kingtones' Sound" was there and Mike's heavy beat was in top form. To show his vocal versatility, Pete sang "My Prayer," which he hadn't done since we started at Porky's. The audience gave him a thunderous applause when he finished. His vocals were fantastic and the crowd responded. The more they clapped and yelled, the more wild we got. The more wild we got, the crazier the audience got. We were magnificent! They screamed! And yelled! Clapped and hooted; they danced like "bee stung savages."

We brought up the African Beatles, but after our mad driving, heart pounding sets, they seemed anticlimactic. The kids didn't get into them and they didn't go over well.

We decided to do *"The Bird"* on our fifth set, while I still had some energy left. Once again it was a huge success. The kids screamed and yelled for encores when we finished. They wouldn't stop! So we decided to bring back "Elvis" one more time. We did "Long Tall Sally." I came out from behind my organ, curled my lip, got my leg and arm in their starting position, and we began. I shook, wiggled, jumped, bounced, did a flip and finally ripped my pants in two. It wasn't just a little rip, my whole bare leg was sticking out and you could see glimpses of my underwear. The whole place was almost in pandemonium by the time we finished the song! The screams were deafening! Of course, they wanted more! Fortunately, we had it planned just right, because it was time for The Percussions to come on stage and thank God they did.

When we took our break, one of the bartenders said he had an extra pair of pants that he kept in the back room. He was nice enough to let me borrow them. While we were waiting to go back on stage, an aristocratic couple came over and introduced themselves to us. They said they really enjoyed our music and invited us over to their mansion for dinner on Tuesday. They suggested that we bring our swimming suites so we could go swimming in their heated kidney shaped swimming pool. All five of us were very excited about this. A free "Fancy dinner!" and a private heated swimming pool appealed to all of us. We thanked them for the invitation and said we would come.

Our last set, needless to say, was anticlimactic. We had put everything into the previous set; we had nothing left. We sounded okay, but the energy that was needed to make our set great was gone.

At the end of the night, when we were getting ready to go, an airline hostess came up to me and said she loved me. She sounded serious. She said I reminded her of Ringo Starr, of the Beatles, and since she couldn't have him, she wanted me. She was 21 years old, had blue eyes and blond hair and was very pretty. She wanted me to go to Miami with her that night. She said she would feed me, put me up for the night, and make love to me. She also said she was well to do and had a lot of money; I could have whatever I wanted. She would not let go of my hand. I told her I was flattered and thanked her for the offer. I said I had a girlfriend in Michigan waiting for me, who I was crazy about, and I could not accept her offer. She finally realized that I wasn't going to go with her and gave up. As she walked away, she told me that I was the greatest and she would see me again.

When I told Bob and Mike about the airline hostess, Bob said I was nuts for not going with her. He said he would have already been in Miami, if she had asked him. We left and went back to our apartment.

Pete and Phil took the same two girls that they had been with for the last couple of nights home again. Pete's girl was very cute, but Phil's girl was just a "plain Jane." I wasn't sure what Phil saw in her, but he was always a little different from us. Whenever we would see a girl with large breast, we would make a big deal about it. But Phil would just say, "Girls are a little like houses; some have big porches and some have small porches; it's what's on the inside that counts." So I assumed that his girl must have been a real sweetheart.

The girls invited Pete and Phil to spend the night with them. Phil decided he wanted to get inside that "house." Although he tried and tried, Jane was very strong and stopped his every move. All Phil got for his trouble was one hour of sleep and nothing more. Pete, on the other hand, was so drunk that he flopped on the bed and passed out. We were all healthy except Mike, who was still fighting a cold. We were getting along well.

March 31, 1964 (Tuesday)

Mike and I got up at 2:30 pm. It was a very nice day outside: 75 degrees and sunny. We were scheduled to go to a fancy dinner that we had been invited to last night, but Pete and Phil had shacked up with the two girls that they had been seeing, and we didn't know how to get a hold of them. Bob, "the blob," was too tired and refused to get up. We had told the couple last night that all of us would come to dinner, and I didn't want to totally disappoint them; so Mike and I went.

When we got there, the couple had their finest china out on the table, set for five people. Mike and I felt like fools. We apologized and said that Pete and Phil had stayed with some friends last night and must have forgotten about the dinner; we didn't know how to get a hold of them. We continued saying, Bob woke up not feeling very well and thought he should not go. We didn't want them to think we were ungrateful, so we lied to them.

Mike and I had a great dinner. We started with an appetizer of shrimp cocktail. This was followed by a lettuce salad topped with almonds, strawberries, mandarin oranges and miniature tomatoes. The main course was filet mignon, twice baked potatoes and steamed broccoli with melted cheese on top. You could cut the steak with your fork. For dessert we had cheesecake with warm raspberry sauce poured over it. It was a meal "fit for a King-*tone!*"

When we finished eating, they wanted us to go swimming. I told them that we didn't bring our suits, but that I had to get back anyway. Mike said that if they didn't mind, he would like to go get his suit and return. They were glad to have him come back.

When we got back to the apartment, Mike grabbed his swimsuit and left. He wasn't gone very long before he returned. He said that their daughter had a few of her girlfriends over swimming; Mike had wanted to impress the girls, so he attempted some kind of a dive off the diving board and hit his head on the bottom of the pool. His neck was very sore and he could hardly turn his head. I put some first aid cream on his neck and massaged it for a half hour.

When Pete and Phil got up, they had totally forgotten about the dinner invitation. They decided to go horseback riding. Someone had given Pete three passes for a free horseback ride. They came back to the apartment before they left, but Pete didn't offer the extra free pass to Bob. Major was a little upset with Pete because of this, until they came back and said they couldn't find the riding stable. They then left and went back to their girls' apartment. They were cooking dinner for them.

We left at 9:15 pm to go to Porky's. The Percussions were going to play the first set that night from 9:30 pm to 10 o'clock. We would go on after them. When we got there, we found Porky's only half full. More and more students were leaving Fort Lauderdale to go back to college. We figured in a few more days, we would be playing to a ghost bar.

We were good that night, but it was very hard for us to get energized with only half the students being there. We did *"The Bird"* early because we had so many requests for it. The audience clapped and cheered when we were done, but once again, having only half as many students, the claps and cheers were much more tame. A little later the students started chanting "The Bird! The Bird!" Since there wasn't a lot going on in the way of dancing, we decided to do it again. After we finished they clapped, cheered and chanted "Birdman, Birdman, Birdman." They had given me another nickname. I was already being called "Ringo" by many of the girls. I guess that was because either I looked a little like Ringo Starr or acted a little like him on stage.

We brought up the African Beatles once again. Their harmonies were great and their choreography was very good. The kids really liked them and clapped and cheered for them when they finished.

When we ended for the night, Phil and I went and gave Porky our two week notice to leave. He tried to talk us out of it. He wanted us to call Tom Johnson, who owned the Coral Gables in Saugatuck, to make sure he wanted us that summer. If he didn't, Porky wanted us to play at his place the whole summer. We didn't tell Porky, but we were not going to call Tom Johnson. Even if Tom didn't want us, we did not want to play at Porky's; we had had enough.

It was good that we were getting ready to go back to Michigan. Being together day and night, everyday, for almost seven weeks was starting to hurt our friendship. Pete was really getting cocky and hard to work with. His favorite saying when he wanted something was, "Don't be a prick." He used that saying quite a bit on Bob because he always wanted to borrow his car. In fact, there were many times that he took Bob's car without even asking him for it. When Major finally suggested that Pete rent his car for a month, Pete said "Kiss ass." It would be good for all of us to get away from each other for a few weeks.

Bob, Mike and I went back to our apartment. Pete and Phil went over to shack up with their two girls once again. We were all healthy except Mike. He had a cold and now a very sore neck. We got along well that day, because all five of us weren't together.

April 1, 1964 (Wednesday)

We woke up at 1:30 pm. We were so tired and worn out, we just lay in bed and watched TV, until we had to go play at the jam session. We thought that this would probably be our last one, because the crowds were getting so small. We finally got up, ate a quick tuna fish sandwich and left for Porky's.

Phil told us he would meet us at the jam session; he would have Pete drop him off when they left the girls' apartment. Pete was going to go back and take a nap at our apartment. He wasn't coming to the jam session because Porky did not want him. Porky said, "Pete does nothing but sit on his ass and drink beer; I don't want him there!" So the four of us played the two hours without him. The crowd was very small, about twenty-five percent of what it had been. They were not really in the mood to party. These were the "die hard" students that didn't want to face the fact that spring break was over. By the size of the crowd that was there, however, it was a fact. We certainly weren't in the mood to play, especially without Pete. We were pretty dead, so was our music and so was the crowd.

When we finished playing, Porky finally paid us for the five jam sessions that we had done. It boiled down to $2.50 an hour per man: Wow! We left and returned to our very dirty apartment. I made supper: Chile and beans. We watched TV until we had to go back to work.

At 8:45 pm, we headed back to Porky's. We did not have a very good night; there were a lot of factors that contributed to it. First of all, we were physically and mentally run down. Then, too, the audience which we drew our energy from, was down to twenty-five percent of the original spring break crowd. Next, Mike's neck was affecting his drumming; even *"The Bird,"* our golden egg in the basket, was a flop. We all knew the end was here, but no one wanted to admit it. When we finished for the night, Porky came over and talked nicely to us. We figured that this was because he wanted us to play at his place during the summer.

Pete and Phil were so tired, they went back to our apartment and not the girls'; they needed sleep. All five of us went to Royal Castle first, and told Homer, the chief cook, waiter and bottle washer, that we would be leaving Florida in about two weeks. He felt bad; he enjoyed us coming there almost every night. He said that he was going to miss us.

Four of us were basically healthy, but run down; Mike was also run down, but he still had a cold and a sore neck. We got along okay that day, but there was tension in the air.

April 2, 1964 (Thursday)

We got up at 4:10 pm. It had been a very nice day outside, but we missed most of it. Phil was trying to learn two more Beatles' songs, the rest of the guys were watching TV, and I fixed supper. This was the first big dinner that I had made in a week. We had steak, mashed potatoes, yellow beans and fried onions.

Our rent was due that day and our landlord wanted to kick us out. Can you imagine that? Just because we had four complaints against us for making too much noise in the early morning hours, he wanted us out!? His wife, however, was an understanding lady that said we could stay for ten more days for $50.00; then we had to get out. We figured we would probably be gone before our ten days were up anyway.

Because we were so tired and worn out, none of us went anywhere that day. We just sat around the apartment and rested. Pete was saying that maybe we should stay at Porky's for the summer. He was only saying that because he had a girlfriend and was hoping to score a home run with her before long. Bob said that he could use the money, so it was okay with him to stay. Phil, Mike and I said that if Pete and Bob wanted to stay, they were on their own. As soon as our obligation to Porky was over, the three of us would be heading for Michigan.

We left for Porky's at 8:45 pm. Because we had rested all day, we were not tired and had some energy. Mike's neck didn't hurt anymore, so he would be back in full swing. As we took to the stage and faced our "down sized audience," we started. You could just feel it. Mike's powerful drum beat was back; Phil and Bob's growling, booming, sound, with their synchronized guitar and bass movements, along with crazy bouncing me, making people laugh and rounding out our sound with my organ, the "Kingtones' Sound" was alive and well! We were back and we were terrific!

Pete was a great showman that night, doing everything in the book to impress his girl. He didn't want Frank, the lead singer of The Percussions, to show him up, and he didn't. The crowd, as small as it was, yelled and clapped after every number. We did *"The Bird,"* and it was great. When we finished the song, they screamed and clapped and chanted "Birdman, Birdman, Birdman." Of course they wanted us to do it again, but we didn't.

We brought up the African Beatles to do their set. They did a good job and the audience liked them.

When we took a break, one customer came over to me and said that we were so much better than The Percussions; that Porky should just have us play there instead of them. I thanked him for the compliment, but then I said that Frank, The Percussions lead singer, was one of the best rock singers I had ever heard, and his band did a decent job behind him. I did think we were better, but The Percussions were very nice young men and worked just as hard as we did; they deserved some respect. Besides, if we would have played every set, without them alternating with us, we would have died.

Pete's and Phil's girlfriends were there all night and they brought a third girlfriend with them. When we finished for the night, Pete came over to me and wanted me to go back to the girls' apartment with him and Phil. Evidently the third girl liked me and wanted to get acquainted. I couldn't believe what I was hearing. Pete knew I was going with Chick and there was no way I was going to mess that relationship up. I simply told him, "No."

Major couldn't believe I turned down another proposition. He said he would have slept with her, even if he had a girlfriend. He just didn't realize how much I loved Chick. So Mike, Bob and I left Porky's on a high! We tooted the horn, waved and screamed out the windows as we left Porky's parking lot. We went to Royal Castle, while Phil and Pete went to their girls' apartment.

When we got back to our apartment, there were two strangers there. As we entered, they quickly introduced themselves as friends of Pete's from Michigan. Pete gave them a key to our apartment so they could crash there for the day. They were returning to Michigan that night. As they got ready to leave, they made all kinds of noise. For a joke, they asked Mike, in a real loud voice, "Hey Mike, do you want to come to Michigan with us?" Mike of course, not thinking, yells back, "Yeah! I'm coming!" We were sure this would be complaint number five to the landlord. We just hoped he would honor our ten day rental. We were all healthy, even Mike, and we got along well that day.

April 3, 1964 (Friday)

We got up at 2:45 pm. It was a nice sunny day: around 72 degrees. Pete's and Phil's girlfriends had set some "sleeping boundaries" for the boys. They could sleep with them, but Pete could not score a "home run," and Phil could not go past "second base." The girls' landlord had found out about the boys sleeping there and said that they could not sleep over anymore. The four of them decided to spend their afternoon at the beach.

Mike went to the beach with some girl he met at Porky's. She had her own car and picked him up at our apartment. They spent most of the afternoon just cruising around in her convertible. She was heading back to Washington D.C. in the morning. Mike had a great time.

Bob and I went shopping. Bob bought a $54.00 twenty-two pistol. I had to buy it for him, because he was not 21; it was illegal to buy a real gun in Florida under the age of 21.

We all got back to the apartment about the same time. I made spaghetti for supper. We watched a little TV and then got ready to go play. We left for Porky's at 8:45 pm. We started to play to more people than what we had on Thursday night, because many of the locals had come in. Once again the "Kingtones' Sound" was there. Mike was at the top of his game playing those drums. Pete's girl was there, so he was extra good, trying to impress her. We did *"The Bird"* and *"Elvis"* and they both received screams, applause and requests to do them again. We held most of the crowd until 3:30 am, which surprised even us. We had another great sounding night.

When we were finished for the evening, Phil and Pete went back to the girls' apartment. I guess they didn't care if the landlord found out. Bob had some girl who latched on to him and wouldn't let him go. She wasn't a bad looking gal, but she was a little on the chubby side. She told Bob that she was going to take him to our apartment and we could go on without him. So Mike and I left and went to Royal Castle. We had just ordered our food, when who should come? It was Bob and "Chubby." We quickly ate and left Bob and his new "Hunka Burnin' Love" in the booth by themselves. We were all healthy and getting along well, because we didn't see each other very much during the day.

April 4, 1964 (Saturday)

We got up at 2:30 pm. It was a rather hot afternoon: 87 degrees. Pete and Phil got up at 3:30 pm. They had spent the night with their girls in their apartment, ignoring the landlord's warning. The boys were not having any luck at "expanding the boundaries" that the girls had made. Bob and I started to watch TV, when what to our surprise, Chubby stopped by. She was all giggles, with lots of hugs for Bob. I asked her if she would like to join us for dinner, as Bob, who was standing behind her was shaking his head no. She said she couldn't; she had just stopped by to say hi. Mike had taken off earlier to Miami to see Lloyd.

I fixed supper of hot dogs and beans. Mike had not come back yet from Miami, so we ate without him. I cleared the table when we were finished, and the boys did the dishes.

When Mike finally got home, we asked him why he was so late. He said, "Let me tell you about my day. When I got to Lloyd's motel, I stopped by the front desk and asked for him. The desk clerk told me he was by the poolside bar, right through the doors behind me. As I rounded the corner to the pool, Lloyd saw me coming and announced me as the drummer at Porky's. The pool deck was packed with spring break kids. Lloyd asked me to run the poolside bar while he went up front for a minute. As I took my position behind the bar, a cute little "built" blond got up from the deck and started to walk (bounce) to the bar. Our eyes met and froze on each other. She had a red, white and blue bikini on and when she sat down, she dropped her breasts on the bar and ordered a beer. I never broke eye contact, leaned back to the cooler, pulled out a beer, opened it and placed it in front of her and said, "It's on the house." Gail Robinson was her name; she wanted to meet Mike at Porky's that night, but didn't have a way to get there. Mike asked Lloyd if he would do him a favor and bring Gail to Porky's later that night. He said he would. The boys were a little envious and wished they had gone to Miami with Mike.

At 8:45 pm, we left for Porky's. We were hoping for another great night; sorry to say, it wasn't. During our second set, Mike broke his bass drum head. It took him the entire set to fix it. In the meantime, The Percussions drummer sat in with us and played his own drums. Not only were his drums not as good sounding as Mike's, but he didn't really know our songs or the beat that went with each of them. Phil tried his best to tell him what the beat should be, but he never quite got it right. It was not a good set.

The Percussions finally came on and we took a break. Mike had been looking for Lloyd and Gail to come in all night. Finally he saw Lloyd; he was so excited he could hardly stand it. His excitement, however, quickly disappeared when Lloyd said that Gail didn't come. Evidently, Gail's girlfriend did not want her to go to Porky's, so they left for their hometown in Canada instead. Mike was crushed.

During our third set, Bob's amp went out. He had to use the other band's bass amp; it changed our sound completely. On our fourth set, there was a big fight in the back of the room; tables and chairs were knocked all over the place. That just about cleared all the customers out of the bar. We brought up the African Beatles and they did do a great job, but there was almost no one there to appreciate them.

This was the last night of playing at Porky's for The Percussions. We were very sad to see them go. We had gotten to know them over the past couple of weeks, and thought of them as friends.

When we finished for the night, Pete and Phil went back to the girls' apartment. Bob, Mike and I stayed for a while at Porky's, and talked to The Percussions as they packed up their equipment to leave. Frank gave me his phone number and said that if we ever made the "Big Time," to please call him. He would love to know someone personally who was famous.

(Note from the author: In the summer of 1964, The Kingtones played at the Coral Gables in Saugatuck, Michigan. Pete got hoarse on a Thursday night and had no voice on Friday. I called Frank in Chicago, to see if he *was available to sing in Pete's place. He was; he took a bus to Saugatuck and sang with us Friday and Saturday night. He did an excellent job. In fact, I think Frank taking Pete's place helped Pete get better quickly. By Sunday, Pete's voice was back, so we said good-bye to Frank and never saw him again.)*

We were not looking forward to Sunday or Monday night, because we were going to have to play all six hours by ourselves. Porky had another band coming in, the Fabulous Apollos, but they didn't start until Tuesday. Because spring break was over, Porky dropped our nights of playing from seven to six. He also dropped our pay to $500.00 for the six nights.

When we got back to our apartment, I hung my suit outside to air out. I suggested that Mike and Bob do the same, because the uniforms were starting to stink. Since we only had the one suit, we had worn those 33 days straight without getting them cleaned. Bob and Pete were healthy, Mike and Phil were getting colds and I was starting to have nose problems. We all got along well that day.

April 5, 1964 (Sunday)

Mike got up at noon and went to Miami to make sure Gail had really left. He couldn't accept the fact that she left without saying good bye. He spent the whole day there with Lloyd and had a good time, but he felt a little blue because she had departed.

Bob got up at 3:30 pm. Chubby had come over and beat on the door. I made Bob get up and answer it. He and Chubby watched TV for a little while, but she got bored and found it more fun to come into my bedroom and pester me until I got up.

Pete and Phil came home around five o'clock. They had spent the night at their girls' apartment, went to the beach for a couple of hours and then came home.

I made hamburgers for dinner; we watched TV until we had to go to Porky's at 8:45 pm. When we got there, we noticed that our name was no longer up in lights on Porky's sign. The African Beatles were now up there. We were very upset about that.

It was a dead night; we had approximately twenty-five people in the whole place when we started. By the time we finished for the night, there were only six people left. We were somewhat apathetic about playing and didn't really try to energize the people. We were mad at the African Beatles, although it wasn't their fault that their name was on Porky's sign; we resented having to back them up. It was a long night.

When we finished our last set and went to get paid, Porky once again stated that if something should happen that we didn't play at the Coral Gables in Saugatuck, he wanted us to come back there and work for him that summer. That did pick up our spirits a little bit.

Mike and Phil were going to go with a couple of girls to watch the sun come up on the beach. Bob, Pete and I went to Royal Castle and then home to bed. Phil and Mike still had colds; the rest of us were healthy. We got along well that day.

April 6, 1964 (Monday)

Mike and Phil came back from their "Sunrise Ceremony" at 8 am. It turned out that Phil didn't have a girl after all; Mike's girl fell asleep and didn't even see the sunrise. Bob, Pete and I got up at 2:15 pm. Pete took off immediately to go see "Pretty Girl," and Phil tagged along to go see "Plain Jane." Mike, Bob and I decided to go to Monkey Jungle in Miami. The day was rather hot, but because we drove in Major's convertible all day, we hardly noticed it.

We caught the very last show before they closed. I felt like I was visiting Tarzan's world. It was a beautiful jungle setting where we were in long screened walkway type cages, and the monkeys ran wild all around us. We had a great time.

We finally left and got back to our apartment the same time Pete and Phil did: 8:30 pm. We got dressed in our uniforms and left for Porky's. We started playing for two people. As the night progressed, people kept coming in until we had a decent size crowd. Since most of the crowd was now local, many of them weren't students and didn't particularly like loud music. A couple of them complained to Porky about our volume and he made us turn down; the "Kingtones' Sound" disappeared.

We were not sounding good and we were not happy about it. We got several requests for *"The Bird,"* but can you imagine Lawrence Welk playing *"The Bird*?" It wouldn't be a pretty sight. So we played it, and it was terrible. The whole night was not good until our last set. At that point, we just didn't care anymore. We started to sing with Pete, we yelled, screamed, jumped around; everything we could think of that was a little crazy. The audience woke up. They liked our energized, crazy set. When we finished, we even got some applause. We didn't realize it at the time, but that would be our last night to ever play at Porky's.

When we left, Pete and Phil went back to their girlfriends' apartment. Phil's girl, Plain Jane, had left Porky's earlier with some other guy. Phil was determined, however, to see if he couldn't somehow get past second base with her. Bob, Mike and I went to Royal Castle and then home.

Mike started to smoke that day. He said it was to help him cut down on eating so much. I thought it was probably to impress Pete and all of his other friends that smoked. I bitched at him for it, but it didn't do any good.

Pete was drinking way too much, and continued to treat the four of us like crap. Bob and Pete were healthy; Phil and Mike had colds and I was starting to get one. The four of us got along great that day.

April 7, 1964 (Tuesday)

We got up at 12:30 pm. It was another hot day: 88 degrees. Pete and Phil were still at their girls' apartment. Mike and I went shopping for a while, but we didn't find anything that we wanted to buy. When we got back, Chubby was there to see Bob. She came up to me and said, "I have something for you." I was expecting to ward off an attempted kiss. She reached into a bag and pulled out an artificial bird mounted on a piece of wood. On it was a name plate saying, "To Bruce – The Greatest Birdman in the Land." What a surprise! I told her thank you, and that I really appreciated it. I said I would keep it forever. *(I still have that mounted bird to this day.)*

Phil and Pete finally came home and we all went to Miami to see Lloyd. We went swimming in his pool, played ball tag and follow the leader; we had a fun time. Mike told us of a great buffet restaurant that was within walking distance of the motel. It had great food and was only 99 cents for all you could eat; so we all went there for lunch. He was correct about the 99 cents, but the food was something else. Some of the chicken dishes looked not done, many of the pasta dishes were over cooked and burnt, the Salisbury steak looked dry and cold, the mashed potatoes..... Well you get the idea! We ate mostly from the salad bar. Mike said it was much better the last time he ate there.

We left Lloyd's and went downtown to shop. Mike and I bought a gun that shot blanks, a starter pistol for races. Phil bought a $10.00 radio, which we saw in another store later on, for $6.00. Pete bought a $10.00 watch that the man said was originally $40.00. We stopped at an auction sale and Bob bought some knives for $1.00, which supposedly cost $9.75. We figured that we probably all were taken, but we had fun shopping. We then went to the movies and saw The Pink Panther. We thought it was hilarious.

After the show, we left Miami and went back to our apartment. Pete went to see Pretty Girl, Mike went to the beach and Phil, Bob and I went to Porky's to see The Fabulous Apollos. When we got there, they were already playing. They were older than we were, but they looked great and sounded very professional. They were real quiet and yet they did rock and roll very well. They did not have the drive or the "kick ass" sound, but Phil thought that they were perfect for Porky's, since spring break was over. After listening to The Apollos for two sets, Phil said he didn't want to play at Porky's anymore. With our volume turned down, he felt The Apollos would make us look bad.

We said hello to Porky and Phil told him that we might not finish out the week. Porky said he understood and we could leave anytime. Bob, of course, wanted to stay because he wanted the money; he didn't care how we sounded, as long as he got paid. Pete wanted to stay because he had a girlfriend there. Mike wanted to stay because Bob and Pete wanted to. I wanted to go because I agreed with Phil and I really wanted to see Chick. We had some heated arguments about staying or leaving. We were all healthy and got along great during the day, but not very well at night.

April 8, 1964 (Wednesday)

We got up at 1:30 pm. The day was very hot and humid: 92 degrees. Pete and Mike decided to go see Lloyd in Miami. Phil worked on his model airplane to finish it up. When he finished it, he was excited to see it fly. He took it outside for its inaugural flight. As it took off, his excitement turned to a puzzled look and then to disappointment as his plane came crashing to the ground. Bob and I went to get some new handles and holsters for our guns: Bob's 22 pistol and my starter gun.

Mike and Pete got back at 6:30 pm. I made hamburgers for dinner and we watched TV until it was time to go to Porky's. We left for Porky's at 8:45 pm. We put on our suits for the 36th time. Even though we tried to air them out, they still smelled a little bit. When we got to Porky's, he had another band playing in our place. Evidently, we had a misunderstanding yesterday, when Phil told him that we might not play out the week. Porky thought that we were not coming back and he hired another band. So that was it: The Kingtones were through at Porky's. We got most of our equipment off the stage, so the other band would have enough room to put their stuff. We would come back tomorrow with the Kingtones' van and pick it up.

We stayed and listened to The Apollos for a while. Pete, who had been drinking for quite a while, got into an argument with Phil. He told Phil that he played his guitar way too loud, and that he was doing us a favor by singing for the same wages that the rest of the band members were getting.

We asked Porky if he would write us a letter of recommendation for other club owners to see. He said he would be glad to. We waited until he had finished it and then went to Royal Castle. We returned to our apartment, packed up a little bit, and just sat around and "shot the bull."

Since we were home early, at least for us, Phil decided he was going to go and try to find a clock and tach for his car. We told him that all the stores were closed. He didn't seem to care. He just took a shopping bag, put a flash light, pliers and screw driver in it, got dressed in all black, and "snuck" out to his car. He left, but came back almost immediately, picking up his wallet. He said he had seen too many movies, where the gangster gets pulled over and he has no wallet. So out the door he went again. Twenty minutes later he was back. He said a cop had pulled him over saying he looked suspicious. He checked out his whole car, but didn't find anything illegal. He told Phil to go straight back to his apartment and stay there. We laughed so hard, our sides hurt.

No one, except maybe Pete, was sad to leave Fort Lauderdale. We liked Porky as a person. He was very nice to us when it came to things that didn't pertain to playing: using his canoe, fishing in his lake, letting Chick come into his club, etc. But as a boss, he was a tyrant and slave driver. We had heard that he had ties to the mafia. Someone asked Phil, "Weren't you afraid of playing for someone in the mafia?" Phil simply replied, "I think as long as you are making money for a guy in the mafia, you'll be okay." We were all healthy and four of us got along well. We were all having a rough time getting along with Pete.

April 9, 1964 (Thursday)

Most of us got up at 9:30 am; we were all thinking of home. Bob got up at 10:30 am. Mike washed The Kingtones' van and Phil washed his car. Pete came home from a night of disappointment and lay down. The rest of us went to Porky's to get our equipment. Boy was our stuff dirty and beat. After loading the equipment into our van, we went back home to finish packing our personal stuff.

We hadn't bought groceries in a week and we almost had no food left. What we did have was bread and mashed potato packets. So I made the boys our last official dinner in our apartment: mashed potato sandwiches. Talk about ungrateful! Geesh! The only ones that would eat it were Bob and I. I have to admit, it wasn't very good, but I pretended that it was delicious. We gave the rest of the condiments, ketchup, mustard, salt, pepper, sugar, etc. to one of the neighbors who hadn't complained about us to our landlord.

This was going to be our last night in Fort Lauderdale, so we wanted to do it up big. Phil and Pete knew that since this was their last night, they both might be able to make a "home run" with their girls. They went to their apartment, dressed and groomed to their finest. When they got there, Pretty Girl had just washed her hair and couldn't go until it dried. So Pete and Phil sat around waiting for her hair to dry. Meanwhile Phil's girl, Plain Jane, went to sleep. After waiting for an hour, Pretty Girl's hair was dry.

Just as they got ready to go, Plain Jane's other boyfriend came over. Pete broke the ice by saying, "Where would you like to go?" Pretty Girl said, "Porky's." Plain Jane said that she was just too tired, so for the three of them to go without her. So Phil, Pete and Pretty Girl all went to Porky's, while tired Plain Jane and her other boyfriend rested on the couch. After staying at Porky's a few hours, the two "Don Juan's" took Pretty Girl back to her apartment, dropped her off and then went home. What an exciting last night for them.

Meanwhile, Bob, Mike and I had our own night of enjoyment. First we went to Porky's to pick up our pay for Monday night's work. We were all excited because this was our final night. We decided to go pay our last visit to the beach and pick up a few souvenirs. The beach area was a ghost town. All the stores were closed and not many lights were on. It made us feel empty inside and gloomy. When we left the beach area, we felt kind of sick and none of us wanted to do anything. So Bob just started driving around for something to do. We finally stopped for gas and Bob realized he needed an oil change. So our exciting night was watching the guy change the oil. When he was done, we returned to our apartment.

Pete and Phil had just arrived at our apartment when we did. Since no one was really tired or wanting to go to bed, we packed the cars and van with our personal things and left, leaving our apartment a total disaster. We stopped at the Royal Castle for the last time and said good bye to Homer. We were all healthy and getting along okay: Michigan here we come!

April 10, 1964 (Friday)

After leaving the Royal Castle, we got on the state highway and headed north. We finally got to US 75, a big beautiful new road. We got on it and went about one mile before the road ended. It was not finished yet. So we got out our map, "recalculated," and started up again. We stopped in Lake City for breakfast; it was excellent. Pete took over driving for Bob to give him a rest. We took detour after detour; we almost went nuts. I almost fell asleep twice while I was driving, but woke up mighty fast when we came to Atlanta, Georgia. If you were sleepy in Atlanta, you had a good chance of ending up dead. The drivers there were crazy; we called it "Wild Man's Land."

We were having some trouble with the van. It would only run if the choke was pulled all the way out; it somehow fixed itself. We hadn't slept all night and were getting very tired. We decided to drive until it started to get dark; we would then get a motel.

We finally stopped. I was sleeping at the time and the guys woke me up to go into the room. As I got out of the van, I thought, "What a dump." We were at a very old, run down motel. Phil said, "We only paid $10.00 for the night, so don't complain, just go to bed." We went to bed at eight o'clock. We were only a few miles from the Tennessee state line. It had been a long, long day. The further north we went, the colder it got. We were all healthy and getting along okay.

April 11, 1964 (Saturday)

We got up at 4:30 am. Our room had little to no heat and we were freezing. We decided rather than go to the office and complain, we would just leave for home. We stopped for breakfast just before Chattanooga; it was not good. My sausage was raw in the middle and my grits were hard; the biscuits were soggy and the cream curdled in Bob's coffee. Needless to say, we went away hungry and not happy.

As we continued on our way, we had to stop for a new tire for the van. The tire was quite worn out and the van was starting to shimmy. We stopped at a garage in Chattanooga and bought a used one for $4.00.

Tennessee had a lot of souvenir fire cracker stores. We stopped at a couple different ones and bought fire crackers. Mike bought a real musket gun that was in very good condition. After we made our purchases, Phil and Mike wanted to get going, so they took off. As we went to our vehicles, and saw their dust fly behind Phil's car, we realized that they went down the wrong road. Bob, Pete and I continued on our way, down the right road. We didn't see Mike or Phil again on our trip home.

We finally stopped at a "restaurant" to eat lunch. It was strictly a vending machine operated restaurant: no waitresses, no cooks, no cashier and no menus. If you didn't have change to put in the vending machine, they had a machine that would turn your dollars into quarters. Then you took the change and put it in the food vending machines. Bob and I were so upset with this modern "Star Trek" restaurant, we refused to buy anything. Pete, however, bought two dishes of macaroni & cheese. Bob and I sat there watching Pete eat; wanting to swallow our pride and eat something also, but no, we weren't going to give in. So we left the restaurant with Pete smiling and full and Bob and I bitching and starving. We finally stopped again in Dayton, Ohio, and ate at a place like Big Boy.

We were so tired of traveling, that we started following trucks that were going over the speed limit, so we could get home quicker. Because we lost Phil, and he was the keeper of the "kitty" money, I was paying for all the gas we put in the van; I kept all the receipts. I figured it would be easier for one of us to collect from Phil, than all three of us.

To the best of my memory, I pulled into Pete's driveway somewhere between 8:00 p.m. and 11:00 p.m. I turned the engine off while Pete gathered up his luggage. When he finally got out and I started up the van, I had a small carburetor fire. I quickly turned the engine off and smothered the small flame. This was not something new for the van; it had happened several times before. I waited three to four minutes and started it up again; this time, no fire.

I can remember saying to myself that I was not going to write into my journal that night. I hated writing in it. I had never kept a journal before our Florida trip, and I never kept one after. I figured some day, as uneventful as it probably was, I would put in the last day's happenings. Over four decades have passed since then, however, and all I can remember of that last night, is what you have just read in the last two paragraphs on these pages.

The Kingtones continued to play for 50 years. But most of those years, would never compare or be remembered, like Spring Break of 1964.

Where Are They Now?

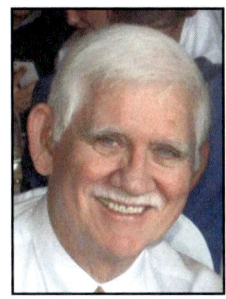

Bruce Snoap continued to play with the Kingtones for 50 years. He and Phil Roberts were together in the band for 48 years. He got married in 1966 to his girlfriend Chick, the love of his life that he had been going with when The Kingtones played at Porky's. At their wedding, Mike King, Bob Major and Phil Roberts were groomsmen. Pete Mervenne, for the first time ever, sang the wedding songs: *Because* and *The Lord's Prayer*. Bruce and Chick have three children and ten grandchildren. They still live in Grand Rapids, Michigan. Although Bruce doesn't see Bob, Mike or Phil much anymore, he still considers them three of his best friends. He has never joined or played music with any other band.

Mike King left the Kingtones when he got married and moved to the East Side of Michigan in 1968. He married a girl that he met while playing with the Kingtones, at a nightclub in Haslett, Michigan. Mike has two children. He worked for the U.S. Army as a mechanical engineer until his retirement in December of 2010. He never joined another band and still lives in Shelby Township, Michigan.

Where Are They Now?

Bob Major had to leave the Kingtones in 1967. He had become a Grand Rapids Police Officer and being a new recruit, had to work nights and had to quit the band. He eventually left the police force to become a security guard for the Amway Grand Hotel and the Grand Rapids Public Library. He retired in 2005. Bob did play bass in two other bands for a short time. In his last band, "Flashback," he was reunited with Pete Mervenne who played drums and sang. Bob has one child and still lives in Grand Rapids, Michigan.

Pete Mervenne got married in 1968 and moved to Flint, Michigan, to work for the *Detroit Free Press*, causing his departure from the Kingtones. He married a girl that he had met at a high school dance in 1962 when the Kingtones played there. He had three children. Pete took up playing the drums and joined a couple of bands for a short time. He, of course, continued to sing, but never received the recognition that he had in the Kingtones. The last band he played in was called "Flashback," where he was reunited with bass player, Bob Major. Pete died in December of 1989 of a massive heart attack while vacationing in Las Vegas; he was 45 years old. The Kingtones had a dance benefit to help raise money for Pete's children for future educational needs.

Where Are They Now?

Phil Roberts stayed in the Kingtones until the band retired in January of 2008. He never joined another band. He owned Mid-Western Sound Recording Studios for several years, where the Kingtones recorded their record *It Doesn't Matter Anymore*; this brought about a three year recording contract with Atlantic Records. Phil's first "love" is Philosophy. He considers himself a philosopher and often attends and even speaks at Philosophy conferences. Phil never married and still resides in East Grand Rapids, Michigan.

In 2010, The Kingtones were inducted into the "Michigan Rock and Roll Legends Hall of Fame." From the "Pete Mervenne Era," 1957 to 1968, L-R: Bruce Snoap, keyboards; Bob Major, bass; Mike King, drums; Phil Roberts, guitar; and Pete Mervenne, lead singer.

The Kingtones Memoirs – 1964

Kingtoneisms

The band that bathes together stays together

I'll marry you tomorrow for a honeymoon tonight.

A song is OK if it does not noticeably suck!

We've been around since the bow and arrow was a secret weapon.

You know you have been playing a long time when you realize your youngest groupie is 60 years old.

Kingtoneisms (Kĭng•tōn•ĭz•əm), n. 1. A phrase, quote or saying that the Kingtones used many times while addressing their audience or an individual.

We can't play an encore because the shuttle is here to take us back to the old folk's home.

Where do I find these guys?

Kingtoneisms

Guys, name this tune and win a free drink – gals, name this tune and win a night with the band!

We have been around so long that we are the only band with a 401k and group health insurance.

Bruce will now pick a song from our song list which is older than the Dead Sea Scrolls.

Here's Crazy George, a voice only a mother could love.

We have a request to play our Big Hit Record. It was #1 for five weeks in a row throughout Michigan and put us where we are today: here at the Harvard Bar.

Here's a song that's not slow or fast, it's half-ass.

Let me remind you folks that we are a dance band; if you are here just to look at us you are not going to get your money's worth. Well look at us, we're not exactly Eye Candy.

Here's the first song I ever learned how to play on the guitar, the Deltones from Lansing, Michigan! "Phil, It's the Bell Notes." "Who?" "The Bell Notes!" "Are you sure?"

Here's a song by one of the many dead people we do.

Kingtones Standard of Excellence, Not Noticeably Bad.

Pictures and Memorabilia

> Jean and Porky Baines
>
> **Porky's Hideaway**
>
> P. O. Box 691 — 3939 N. Federal Hwy.
> OAKLAND PARK, FLORIDA
>
> To Whom It May Concern:
>
> I have had the Kingtones in my nite club for the last six weeks. In my opinion they are a very excellent Rock N' Roll Band, in which they feature a very talented singer. The boys are very congenial, and punctual. I would recommend them very highly to any other nite club owner who desires a fine young band.
>
> Donald (Porky) Baines

A letter recommending The Kingtones from Donald "Porky" Baines.

Influenced by The Beatles uniforms, The Kingtones outfitted themselves with imported Nehru suits, including shoes from Italy.

Bob Major (Bass) age 20

Mike King (Drums) age 18

Bruce Snoap (keyboards) age 21

Phil Roberts (Guitar) age 20

The Kingtones Memoirs – 1964

Pete Mervenne, The Kingtones lead singer, age 20.
A charismatic teen idol and heartthrob; the ultimate in cool.

In 1964, Porky's Hide Away became the number one college nightclub to go to because of The Kingtones.

During Spring Break, if you didn't get to Porky's at least an hour early, you couldn't get in for lack of room.

The Kingtones Memoirs – 1964

The Kingtones were so proud to have their name in lights,
that Porky let them put their own name on his sign.

102   *The Kingtones Memoirs – 1964*

Pete was known as the man with the "Stainless Steel Vocal Chords" with Phil Roberts on guitar. Pete was also a master at calling the right songs at the right time. Bob Major playing bass.

Although Bruce seldom did lead singing, "Surfin' Bird" was an exception and one of The Kingtones most requested songs. Bob Major, Phil Roberts and Mike King in the background.

Left picture: Bruce doing his mock impression of Elvis for the Kingtones rendition of "Long Tall Sally." Right picture: Mike King, the driving force behind The Kingtones sound and Bruce Snoap, their extroverted keyboard player.

Picture above: With over one hundred songs in their repertoire, The Kingtones were a very current top 40 Rock 'N Roll band. From left to right, Bob Major, Phil Roberts, Bruce Snoap, Mike King.

Right picture: Bob Major, former sax player turned bass player.

The Kingtones Memoirs – 1964

When the "Kingtones Sound" was at its best, the dancers went crazy.
Phil on guitar, Bruce on keyboards, Pete singing, and Bob on bass.

Billy, Lillie, and the Thunderbirds were a class act from Las Vegas.

The Kingtones Memoirs – 1964

Porky's small "pirate ship" was to attract customers to come in and see what his place was all about.

Bruce, Bob and Mike exploring the swimming pool behind Porky's nightclub.

The Kingtones Memoirs – 1964

Bruce and Phil fishing in Porky's man-made lake during their day off.

With two 89¢ fishing poles, Phil and Bruce caught 15 bluegills.

The Kingtones Memoirs – 1964

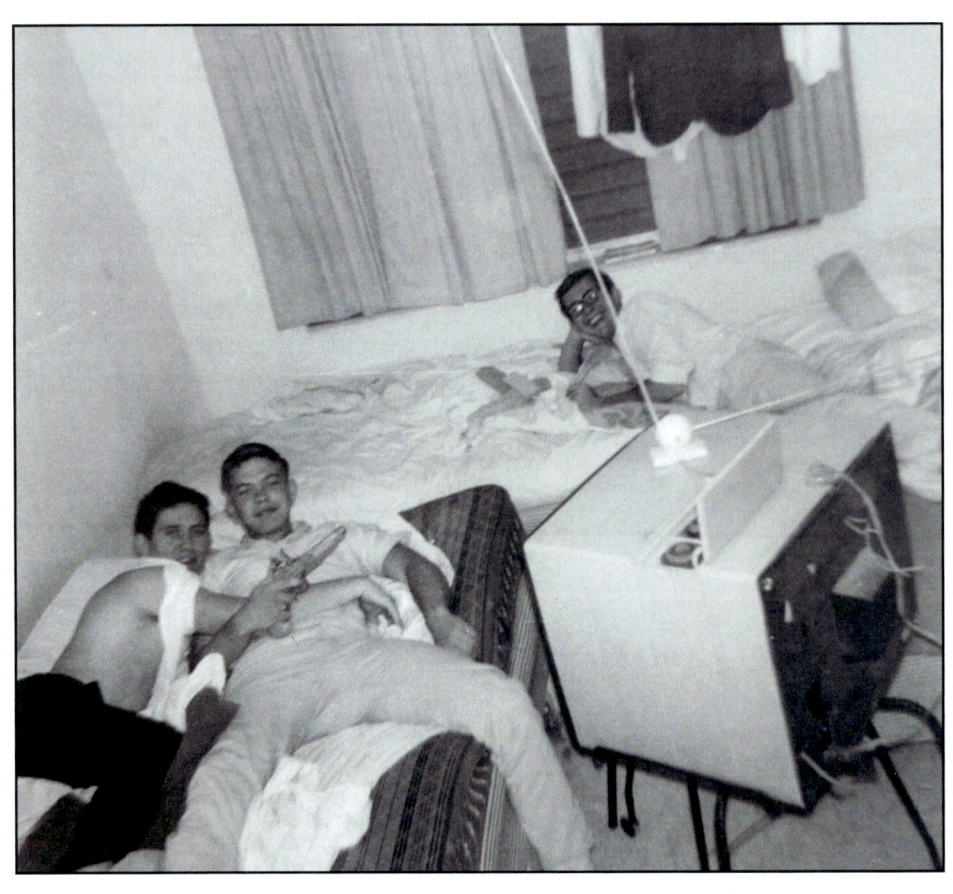

Because their apartment was so small, Bruce, Bob, Phil and Mike (not shown), all shared the same bedroom.

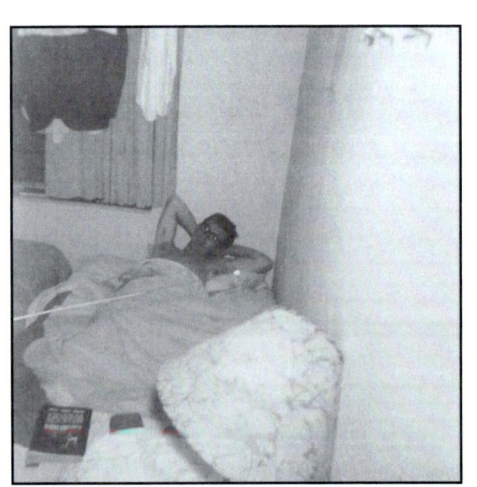

The Plantation Apartments were single unit buildings where The Kingtones stayed for two months while playing at Porky's.

Mike, Bob, and Bruce taking in the shows and exhibits at the Miami Seaquarium, one of the largest marine-life attractions in the world in 1964.

The Kingtones Memoirs – 1964

On April 6, 1964, three days before The Kingtones returned to Michigan, Bruce, Bob, and Mike went to Monkey Jungle in Miami.

1964 – Porky's

The Kingtones continued to play for 50 years. But most of those years, would never compare or be remembered, like Spring Break of 1964. (L to R) Phil Roberts (guitar), Mike King (drums), Pete Mervenne (lead singer), Bruce Snoap (keyboards), Bob Major (bass).